Imagination and Time

Imagination and Time

Mary Warnock

BLACKWELL

Oxford UK & Cambridge USA

Copyright © Mary Warnock 1994

The right of Mary Warnock to be identified as author of this work has been asserted in accordance with the Copyright, Designs and Patents Act 1988.

First published 1994
Reprinted 1996

Blackwell Publishers Ltd
108 Cowley Road
Oxford OX4 1JF
UK

Blackwell Publishers Inc.
238 Main Street
Cambridge, Massachusetts 02142
USA

British Library Cataloguing in Publication Data

A CIP catalogue record for this book is available from the British Library.

Library of Congress Cataloging-in-Publication Data

Library of Congress data has been applied for

ISBN 0–631–19018–X
0–631–19019–8 (pbk)

Typeset in 11 on 12½ pt Sabon Symposia by Apex Products, Singapore
Printed in Great Britain by Athenæum Press Ltd, Gateshead, Tyne & Wear

This book is printed on acid-free paper

'I believe that order is better than chaos, creation better than destruction. I prefer gentleness to violence, forgiveness to vendetta. On the whole I think that knowledge is preferable to ignorance, and I am sure that human sympathy is more valuable than ideology. I believe that in spite of the recent triumphs of science, men haven't changed much in the last two thousand years; and in consequence we must try to learn from history. History is ourselves... And I think we should remember that we are part of a great whole, which for convenience we call nature. All living things are our brothers and sisters. Above all, I believe in the God-given genius of certain individuals, and I value a society that makes their existence possible.'

Kenneth Clark
Civilisation

Contents

Preface

This book is a version of two separate but somewhat over-lapping sets of lectures, the Gifford Lectures, delivered in the University of Glasgow in the spring of 1992, under the title *Imagination and Understanding*, and the Read–Tuckwell lectures, delivered in the University of Bristol in the autumn of the same year, entitled *Human Immortality*.

I owe a great debt of gratitude, first, to the electors to the Gifford Lecturership. I was very much aware of the honour done to me and of the great line of lecturers in whose footsteps I trod. I am also very grateful to the University of Glasgow for their unfailing hospitality, and to those members of the University and of the general public who loyally formed my audience.

I am equally indebted to the electors to the Read–Tuckwell Lecturership, and to the University of Bristol, especially the Philosophy Department. The topic of the lectures I delivered there is laid down, in the terms of the benefaction, as human immortality. Such a subject allowed me the unusual oppor-tunity to consider the relations between religious and phi-losophical thought. I do not mean by this that I treated the Philosophy of Religion. My interest was rather in those areas where theology and philosophy overlap in their concerns, just as, in writing about Imagination, in any context whatever, it seems to me of great interest to consider the areas where literature and philosophy overlap. In addition, I must express my gratitude to the Leverhulme Foundation for awarding me an Emeritus Fellowship, for two years, during which time I have prepared my lectures for publication. I have greatly appreciated their generosity.

The Gifford Lectures must, according to the terms of the trust, touch on subjects related to morals or theology; the Read–Tuckwell Lectures, as I have said, must have human immortality as their subject. In this book, chapters 6 and 8 come more or less directly from the Read–Tuckwell lectures; the remaining chapters are an edited version of the Gifford Lectures, with some material added from the other lectures. Both sets of lectures are, by the terms of the lecturership, intended for the general public, and therefore must attempt to address a non-professional audience. This imposed on me a duty to try to be as clear and direct as the subject-matter permitted, and to assume little or no previous philosophical knowledge. It also gave me an excuse to range widely over what, in purely academic terms, would be thought to be different disciplines. Within professional philosophy it has been difficult, in the last fifty years or so, to cross boundaries between one branch of the subject and another, within the covers of one book. It has been still more difficult to stray into what have come to be considered totally different academic subjects, literature, for example, or theology. This is, in one very important respect, right; for no one can any longer claim to be a polymath; and to talk about what you do not thoroughly understand is, in general, disgraceful. However, I used my audience, drawn from different parts of the universities or from outside them, as an excuse to breach these rules. I did so the more willingly because I believe that the boundaries between one discipline and another, though usually essential, can sometimes be inhibiting. I do not argue that there should not exist specialization, or true and detailed scholarship; on the contrary those who, like me, are neither specialists nor scholars depend entirely on the existence of those who are. I would simply argue that scholarship and proper academic concern for the pursuit of truth within one field are not harmed by occasional forays into surrounding territories.

Ever since I first began to think about philosophy, as an undergraduate, and while I was still at school, I have always loved and admired those philosophers, such as Plato, Spinoza and Kant, who seemed to deduce a moral theory from something much more grand and universal than morality itself. And I suppose that no moral theory could be worth much if it were not derived from some general ideas about the nature of man,

the significance of his relatively brief individual life, and his
relation to the universe as a whole. So I need not apologize
for trying, on an extremely small scale, to link ideas about
human perception and understanding with those imaginative
constructions that make us aware of the past and the future,
and induce a sense of what is worth doing or worth having,
the values we ascribe to things. I have tried to suggest that we
cannot keep knowledge and understanding in a separate com-
partment from liking and disliking, seeking and avoiding, fearing
or loving, in a word from values. Both are equally dependent on
imagination. This, broadly, was the theme of my lectures.

In straying so widely over different areas of philosophy, and
beyond, I have pursued a partly historical thread. This is, in my
case, unavoidable. My interest in philosophy has always been
an interest in the history of ideas. (This is far from always
true of professional philosophers.) But, in so short a space, my
history is necessarily extremely selective. Moreover, in talking
about the present, I may seem to make unjustified assumptions
about how 'we' (present people) think, in contrast with how
'they' (past people) thought. I can only say that my interpretation
of what 'we' think is naturally my own, though not particularly
original; and I acknowledge that there could be other ways of
presenting the facts. It is indeed part of my thesis that different
accounts can he given of history. But it is also part of this thesis
that not just any account will do. I hope that what seems coherent or explanatory to me will seem so to at least some others.
If not, it is for others to tell a better story, interpreting the
past in a different way, and producing greater understanding. I
would add only that my story has a moral. It points, in the end,
to the urgent need to preserve and pass on, through education,
some of those enduring values that can be conceived by imagination, and whose worth can be understood and shared with other
people, both now and in the future. And so my final chapter has
a practical purpose: it makes recommendations for education,
of a limited, but, it seems to me, an all-important kind. It is
not enough to aim for what relativist critics and philosophers
call 'truth of a kind'. In order to restore to them a sense of the
point or significance of their lives, it is necessary so to enlarge
the imagination of children while they are still at school (and
of adults after they have left school) that they can feel the

significance of their own lives. They need to be enabled to take on for themselves the values which alone give meaning to what they are doing and what they will do, so that they may form part of a society in which the imagination, and especially the imagination of genius, can continue to flourish for as long as we can look into the future, and beyond.

Mary Warnock
Axford

1

Introduction: The Inner and the Outer World

In addressing the topic of Imagination, I have entered a field that is not only very ancient, but increasingly well trodden. The relation between the imaginative and the rational, the fictitious and the true has occupied philosophers certainly since Plato. Moreover poets have perforce entered the debate, sometimes to claim that imagination can alone give rise to true under-standing, sometimes to defend its separation from the factual and the scientific. Imagination, these latter argue, is free and is not bound to imitate Nature. So Sir Philip Sidney, following the Italian literary critics of the sixteenth century wrote

> Only the poet, disdaining to be tied by any subjection, ...
> lifted up with the vigour of his own invention, doth grow in
> effect another nature, in making things either better than nature
> bringeth forth, or, quite anew, forms such as never were in
> nature, as the Heroes, Demigods, Cyclops, Chimeras, furies and
> such like: so he goes hand-in-hand with nature, not enclosed
> within the narrow warrant of her gifts, but freely ranging only
> within the zodiac of his own wit. (*Defence of poetry*, ed. J. A.
> Van Dorston, OUP, 1966)

But can such wonderful inventions give us insight, or only pleasure? Can they be thought to lead us towards understand-ing and truth? This is the primary question which this book addresses.

The eighteenth century marked a turning point in the history of ideas, nowhere more obviously so than in the theory of the imagination. M. H. Abrams has argued persuasively that during this time the prevailing metaphor of the mind as a whole changed from that of a mirror slavishly reflecting the world (though with some exceptions, in the genius of poets) to that of a lamp, illuminating by its own inner brilliance that world outside on which it shines (M. H. Abrams, *The Mirror and the Lamp: Romantic Theory and the Critical Tradition*, OUP, 1960). But, as is the way with generalizing metaphors, this one can be understood only by reference to specific examples. I want to start by considering the philosophical background to this change, in order to see what it entails. We, in the late twentieth century, cannot go back. The lamp image seems to fit us best, but we need to examine what this entails.

And so our first question must be about the nature of the illumination that the lamp throws onto the world. And a further question is suggested by the first: who is the lamp-bearer? If the eighteenth century changed the concept of imagination, it also began to change that of the self, the single, continuous, identical person whose life-history was of interest, sometimes of overwhelming interest, to himself and others. The idea of life, a life which is someone's to lead, (a βιος in the Greek language, not mere ζωη such as is shared by plants and other animals as well as men) is my other main concern in what follows. For the idea of a life in this sense is inseparable from that of time. To lead a human life, a man must have a notion of himself as having a past and a future. Now, as I shall argue later, it is an essential feature of imagination that it enables us to think about things that are absent, including things which no longer exist or do not yet exist. It is thus only through imagination that a man has a concept of himself as having a history which is not yet finished. So the bearer of the illuminating lamp must be a figure in time, remembering what is past, and foreseeing how things might be in the future. This is the second part of my subject.

First, then, I must discuss some features of the post-eighteenth century concept of imagination. I want to consider it as it bears on the relation between the inner and the outer world, the 'I', on the one hand, who thinks and imagines, and, on the other hand, the world at large, which he seeks to understand, and his grasp of general truth about that world. It is, as I have said, familiar ground; but it is too often trodden separately by historians of art or literature on the one side, and historians of philosophy or practising philosophers on the other. It is my view that these enquirers should tread it together, and that they should help each other (however tiresome this may be for librarians, publishers and others who want to codify kinds of book in tidy categories). Those whose primary interest is in the philosophy of mind or moral philosophy, should be more ready than they sometimes are to listen to those whose concern is primarily with the arts. One incidental consequence of such a cooperative approach is that the outcome might perhaps become intelligible to a larger number of people than those who generally tangle with either philosophy or criticism, in the narrow sense. There are those who are deterred by arguments too manifestly 'specialist', and who feel unable to enter a discussion or criticize an argument in such a context. Yet philosophy, at least, ought to be able to offer itself for such criticism, wherever it is feasible to do so. There are many points of view from which one may survey the whole historical scene. But it might be generally agreed that the history of Western Philosophy from the seventeenth century until the mid-twentieth century, at least that part that was concerned with the nature of knowledge, can be seen as a long drawn-out attempt to shake off the shackles of Cartesianism. Descartes had argued that the mind and the body were two totally distinct substances, the one mysteriously accommodated, at least temporarily, within the other. My body is a physical object, and it is equipped with organs of sense which react to the world it inhabits. My mind, in contrast, is a mental entity, full of ideas that are not physical objects. How do physical and physiological reactions translate themselves into a wholly new kind of thing, a mental entity, such as my idea of redness or of a loud noise? If I have one of these ideas at a particular moment, how do I know whether it bears any relation to anything outside my own consciousness? How can I assure myself that the idea of an external world, waiting to be explored, is not simply a construction of my imagination, a dream?

Descartes solved his problem in a rather high-handed way, by finding in his consciousness a number of innate ideas, which he argued could not have got in there from outside, or 'adventitiously'. Among these innate ideas was the idea of a benevolent God, who would not allow his creatures to be deceived into thinking there was an external world if there was not. And so we can assume that all our apparent knowledge of the world, and the whole structure of science is to be relied upon, provided only that we take care, at each stage of our progress in understanding, to break down our experiences into manageable parts, checking our observations accurately, and not going beyond what we clearly and distinctly perceive. For clarity and distinctness in the ideas themselves are the criteria of truth, whether we are concerned with innate or 'adventitious' ideas. We can inspect our ideas, and find out how clear and how distinct they actually are as they present themselves to us. (See for example 'Rules for Direction of the Understanding', especially Rules XII and XIII, in *The Philosophical Works of Descartes*, tr. Haldane and Ross, CUP, 1931, vol. 1, pp. 35–54). Thus, the distinction between the world of ideas in the mind and the material world outside was maintained; but it was ultimately innate ideas, given us at birth and in no way dependent on outside stimuli, which had priority and upon which science and understanding were founded. Such methods did not satisfy the British Empiricists, who shared Descartes' presumption that mind and body were two different worlds (if not two different substances), but could not reconcile themselves to the notion that knowledge could come from any source other than the senses. Their problem was therefore even more intractable than his. They refused to extricate themselves by means of the device of innate ideas. In briefly tracing the history of the attempts to make sense of the great divorce between the mental and the physical, the inner and the outer worlds, I shall in passing, refer to both John Locke (1632–1704) and George Berkeley (1685–1753). But I shall concentrate especially on David Hume (1711–76), who constructed a theory within which the imagination became the sole bridge between the two worlds, and who is therefore highly relevant to my subject, as well as occupying a crucial place in the history of philosophy.

The first two books of Hume's *Treatise of Human Nature* were published in 1739, the third book, 'On Morals', in the following year. The first book 'Of the Understanding' was concerned primarily with the great Cartesian question I have just outlined: how the inner and the outer worlds are related. Hume held, just as Descartes and Locke had before him, that our sensory experiences, seeing, hearing, even touching, are essentially inner experiences, impressions which each one of us separately receives. Hume divides all 'mental' activities or experiences into two kinds: impressions and ideas. Under the title impression

'I comprehend', he says, 'all our sensations, passions and emotions, as they make their first appearance in the soul. By ideas I mean the faint images of these in thinking and reasoning' (*Treatise of Human Nature*, Bk I, Pt I, sec. I, ed. Selby-Bigge, Clarendon Press, 1888). 'The difference betwixt these', he says, 'consists in the degree of force and liveliness with which they strike upon the mind'. And he goes on: 'I believe it will not be very necessary to employ many words in explaining this distinction. Everyone of himself will readily perceive the difference betwixt feeling and thinking'. In choosing the word 'impression' to refer to our mental experiences, including those which we take to be experiences 'of' an outer world, it might be thought that Hume has given the game away. For an 'impression' suggests that a mark is impressed on an object by an outer force, as a crest may be impressed on hot sealing wax by a signet ring. If this were implied, then Hume would have to admit that at least some of our impressions carry a reference to something other than themselves, namely to that agent which makes the impression on our mind. But he is careful to explain that this is not so. In a footnote to this section (ibid., p. 2) he says 'By the term of impression, I would not be understood to express the manner in which our lively perceptions are produced in the soul, but merely the perceptions themselves; for which there is no particular name either in English or any other language, that I know of'. (One might be inclined to argue that there is no particular name, simply because there is no particular sense to be made of a 'sensation' of redness, say, or of roughness or smoothness which has no reference to anything but a mental experience.) At any rate, if you and I and every individual have each our own sense impressions, and if the language we use is originally designed to refer to these impressions, the question arises how we can communicate with each other. For impressions are all that we 'have'. And we each 'have' them privately. Yet we do communicate, and it is plain from the success we have in doing so that we and other people share a common world which we inhabit together, and can talk about. Hume recognized, as his predecessors had not, what a trap his empiricist theory had led him into. He deployed the concept of imagination in large measure to extricate himself from this trap.

He invoked imagination in at least three ways, to explain our common understanding of the world. All our experience of the world came, as we have seen, from impressions, that is from sense experiences and other inner sensations. But besides this we have ideas, which are formed in the mind either by reason or by imagination, and are related to impressions in the sense that they are mental copies or shadows of them. So in the first place, he regarded imagination as the reproductive faculty by which we are enabled to recreate in ourselves, in the form of ideas, experiences we have once had immediately, through impressions. So if I recall a delicious meal, though I have no present impressions, yet I have, in Hume's words, 'faint images' of these impressions, and these are what he calls 'ideas'. Thus the imagination, or image-making faculty, essentially enables us to think about things that are not present to us now.

It is worth remarking that Hume here makes no distinction between imagination and memory. It is the function of imagination, he says, to enable us to relive the past. Equally, though he is less interested in this, it enables us, up to a point, to anticipate the future. Its central function is to think about things in their absence, through copies or faint images of them. Later in the *Treatise*, Hume expends considerable efforts on trying to distinguish the ideas of memory from those of imagination, and in the end comes up with the less than satisfactory criterion for distinction, that ideas of memory are more vivid than those of imagination, and command belief. Belief itself is defined in terms of a certain compelling vivacity by which we are forced to assent to something we present to ourselves. 'When we remember any past event', he says, (ibid., I, I, III, p. 9) 'the idea of it flows in upon the mind in a forcible manner; whereas in the imagination the perception is faint and languid, and cannot without difficulty be preserved by the mind steddy and uniform for any considerable time'. Later he expands this:

A painter, who intended to represent a passion or emotion of any kind, wou'd endeavour to get a sight of a person actuated by a like emotion, in order to enliven his ideas and give them a force and vivacity superior to what is found in those which are mere fictions of the imagination... Thus it appears that the belief or assent, which always attends the memory and the senses is nothing but the vivacity of those perceptions they present; and that this alone distinguishes them from the imagination.

Intrinsically, however, the ideas of memory and those of imagination are the same. And with this, in my view, we ought to agree. For memory, like imagination, enables us to think about that which is not, or is no longer, the case, or which we are not or are no longer now experiencing. Memory should be regarded as a sub-class of imagination, not as a wholly separate 'faculty'.

Hume gave imagination a second role which introduced that idea of freedom invoked by poets such as Sidney, when they think of the creativity of the imagination. Imagination enables us to bring together a number of different impressions we have had in the past, in order to make up general, even abstract, ideas. If I see or hear the word 'dog' I may by a habit of imagination bring together a thought, not just of my dog Fido alone, but of dogs as a whole. I may use the image of the particular to stand for the general. I can imaginatively see through the particular characteristics of Fido to the nature of the dog as a species. And if I am tempted to argue that, for example, all dogs have short legs, on the ground that Fido has short legs, my imagination can even provide me with counter-examples, enabling me to produce the idea of an Afghan hound to undermine my rash generalization. Hume does not tell us how this is possible. It is simply a function that the imagination has to produce relevant images. He says, with resignation, 'To explain the ultimate causes of our mental actions is impossible' (ibid., I, 7, pp. 20, 21).

A third and crucial role of the imagination in Hume's theory is that which it exercises when objects of sense are actually before us. He believed that our perception of the world consists of a number of discrete and short-lived impressions, derived from all of our senses, but separate and in themselves suggesting nothing beyond the immediate moment when we receive them, the fragments from which a kaleidoscope is made up, but with no unifying framework within which a pattern might appear. He was obliged therefore to ask how it is that we seem to ourselves to perceive a world that is continuous, full of objects with an existence of their own, relatively enduring and relatively predictable. We distinguish, in real non-philosophical life, between momentary sensations which we would claim as 'ours', itches, prickings, aches and pains, feelings which we rightly believe would not exist unless we were there to experience them and, on the other hand, perceptions. These are intrinsically different from sensations, and are derived, as we inevitably believe, from objects which exist out there, waiting to be perceived. We locate them, not in parts of our bodies, but outside us. They are independent of us, and so perception seems, inevitably, to be perception of external objects which are objects of our attention. If all our experience is a series of fleeting impressions how can we draw such a distinction as that between sensation and perception? Here is the point at which Hume and the other empiricists have to grapple with the problem left them by Descartes, whose own solution they had rejected. How can we explain our relation to the outside world? What does it mean to distinguish inner from outer experience? It is in trying to answer this question that Hume seriously calls on the notion of imagination.

His answer is contained in the section of the *Treatise* entitled 'Of Scepticism with regard to the Senses' (ibid., I, IV, 2, pp. 187–218). He is concerned here not with the question how we come to form general ideas, say of dogs, but how we come to form the idea of a particular dog, Fido, who is seen and heard by us over and over again. Why do we believe that Fido has a life of his own, entering and re-entering our life only sporadically? The central concept here is that of continuity through time. If we can see reason to believe in the continuity of an object, any object; if, that is to say, we can show that it does not flick in and out of existence every time we turn our attention to it or away from it, but exists continuously through a period of time, then we have accounted also for our belief in its independence from ourselves and its distinctness of existence. This will be enough to justify a belief in the 'externality' or 'publicity' of the world, not mind-dependent, but having its own temporal existence. And so the distinction between sensation and perception will be justified.

Hume believed that there were only three faculties of the mind which could be responsible for our belief in the continuity of objects in the outside world, a belief which he would not deny that we possess. These were our senses, our reason and our imagination. He regarded it as absolutely obvious that the senses could not give rise to such a belief. And indeed this follows from his theory of the nature of perception. For the impressions we receive through the senses are themselves discontinuous. We are always blinking, or going to sleep or going away. We could not possibly have Fido under our eye all the time. If we had nothing but our senses to rely on we would believe the world to be full of discontinuous items. But we do not believe this. Hume's arguments against the responsibility of reason for our belief in continuity are more confusing. Reason, in his use of the term, means abstract reasoning such as forms the basis of mathematics or logic; and his main argument against the ability of reason to assure us of the continuous and separate existence of the external world is that everybody presumes that such a world exists. Children and peasants, who are incapable of following a proof, nevertheless assume that there are objects such as dogs which have each their own history and can be identified and re-identified as Fido. They do not reason in favour of this belief; they just assume it. So if reason is not at the root of their conviction, it cannot be at the root of anyone's. This, it need hardly be said, is a poor argument. For those who cared to try might be able to produce a proof of something that everyone else took for granted without proof. Some of the propositions of elementary mathematics might be of this kind. Nevertheless, Hume uses it as an argument to show that there is nothing left but imagination that can possibly be responsible for our belief in the continuity and therefore the externality of the world.

Imagination is said by Hume to perform the feat of making us believe that the world is peopled by continuous and independent objects by filling in the gaps in our actual experience. For the imagination, he says, 'when set into any train of thinking is apt to continue even when its object fails it, and, like a galley put in motion by the oars, carries on its course without any new impulse' (ibid., p. 198). Now impressions of Fido, though discontinuous, are related to each other by similarity. Imagination completes the uniformity by filling up the gaps in our experience with a fictitious idea of the object existing even when we are not experiencing it, for, as we have seen, imagination creates ideas out of what we *have* had impressions of in the past. It is by means of imagination that we recognize the house we see today as identical with the house we saw yesterday, the very same house. Imagination can produce ideas by which we can link yesterday's house with today's. When Fido comes in we greet him as an old friend because we have not only a memory-idea of him before he went out, and a present impression of him now he has come back and stands before us. We can by imagination have ideas of him while he was away. And this is, it seems, how we necessarily think, in cases of impressions linked as ours of Fido are, by similarity.

However, Hume was not pleased with this solution. It was forced on him by his implicit faith in there being three and only three faculties involved in our understanding of the world, reason, sense and imagination; by his narrowly mathematical concept of reason; and, worst of all, by his assumption that sense gives us access only to internal discontinuous and discrete impressions, not the external world. If we take it for granted that there is an external world, he was bound to argue that such a concept was a concept of the imagination. And yet he retained the commonly held view that imagination is a pretty poor thing, certainly not fit to be relied on for such a momentous responsibility as that of furnishing the world with those solid separate objects which we all assume are its proper furniture. At the end of the section on scepticism he says 'I cannot conceive how such trivial qualities of the fancy, conducted by such false suppositions can ever lead to any solid or rational system'. And he concludes that there is no cure for scepticism: 'carelessness and inattention alone can afford us any remedy' (ibid., p. 218). Nevertheless there seem to have been other moods in which Hume was more confident of the powers of the imagination. In Part IV section 4 of the first book of the *Treatise* he says (ibid., p. 225)

'I must distinguish in the imagination betwixt the principles which are permanent, irresistable and universal; such as the customary transition from causes to effects, and from effects to causes: And the principles which are changeable, weak and irregular... The former are the foundation of all our thought and actions, so that upon their removal human nature must

immediately perish and go to ruin. The latter are neither unavoidable to mankind, nor necessary or even useful in the conduct of life... For this reason the former are accepted by
philosophy, the latter rejected.

How does Hume claim to know which operations of the
imagination are irresistable and, as he puts it 'just' and which
are not? How are we supposed to distinguish the necessary,
common and universal principles upon which we may rely from
the whimsical, fanciful or idiosyncratic? He has no real answer
to this question. The concluding section of Book I (ibid., Pt IV,
sec. 7, p. 265) contains his most serious attempt to answer
it. He raises the question in a quite general form: 'Can I be
sure... that I am following truth; and by what criterion shall
I distinguish her, even if fortune shou'd at last guide me on
her footsteps?' His answer is as follows:

After the most accurate and exact of my reasonings I can give
no reason why I shou'd assent to it; and feel nothing but a
strong propensity to consider objects *strongly* in that view under
which they appear to me. Experience is a principle which in-
structs me in the several conjunctions of objects for the past.
Habit is another principle, which determines me to expect the
same for the future; and both of them conspiring to operate
upon the imagination, make me form certain ideas in a more
intense and lively manner than others which are not attended
by the same advantages. Without this quality, by which the
mind enlivens some ideas beyond others (which seemingly is so
trivial, and so little founded upon reason) we cou'd never assent
to any argument nor carry our view beyond those few objects
which are present to our senses. Nay even to those objects we
cou'd never attribute any existence, but what was dependent
on the senses; and must comprehend them entirely in that succession of perceptions which constitutes our self or person. Nay
further, even with relation to that succession, we cou'd only
admit of those perceptions which are immediately present to
our consciousness, nor cou'd those lively images, with which
memory presents us be ever receiv'd as true pictures of past perceptions. The memory, senses, and understanding are, therefore,
all of them founded on the imagination, or the vivacity of our
ideas.

As with belief itself, there is no criterion of truth except 'viva-city' of ideas. There seems to have been little advance beyond Descartes' criterion of 'clarity and distinctness'. And this con-clusion leads Hume back directly both to his scepticism, and his despair. The only consolation he has is that 'since reason is in-capable of dispelling these clouds, nature herself suffices to that purpose'. His philosophical melancholy is temporarily cured: 'I dine, I play a game of back-gammon, I converse and am merry with my friends; and when after three or four hours' amusement I wou'd return to these speculations, they appear so cold, strain'd and ridiculous that I cannot find it in my heart to enter into them any farther'. (ibid., p. 269).

Hume, then, has placed the imagination in a pivotal role. It is necessary both to our thinking of things when they are not present to our senses, and to our thought of them when they are so present, if we are to imbue these objects of perception with any permanence or any existence separate from ourselves, the perceivers. Without imagination we should be lost; for only with its help can we interpret our experience, turn it into ex-perience of an outer world, and thus make use of it in under-standing what and where we are, and what we need to do. Yet he left the central problem unsolved. If imagination, the think-ing of what is not, or what is unreal or merely possible, is essential to our knowledge of the real external world, how are we to distinguish knowledge from fake-knowledge, truth from fantasy? Can the imagination ever give rise to knowledge? Is this not a contradiction? What is the relation of imagination to truth, of our inner fantasies to the way things really are out there? As long as he failed to answer this question, the mystery of how we can talk to one another about an apparently common world must remain a mystery.

The history of philosophy is often thought of as divided into 'pre-Kantian' and 'post-Kantian' philosophy; and rightly, because Immanuel Kant (1724–1804) seems to have been the first truly professional philosopher. He fully understood the trap into which Hume and other empiricists had fallen, and set about, in the *Critique of Pure Reason*, to try to get them out of it, and to establish a basis for our belief in the possibility of genuinely and communally knowing a world external to ourselves. Kant distinguished between the empirical and the *a priori* imagination.

The empirical imagination was able to fill our minds wi
images, which particular images depending on what we each
individually happened to have experienced in our lives. The
a priori imagination, on the other hand was, he held, the same
for all of us. It works in a complex way. We, rational human
beings, in virtue of our rational nature, are in possession of
certain laws which we necessarily apply to the data given us
through our senses. Thus we order our sense data into before and
after, into groups which make up substantial and independent
objects in space, into causal sequences. Kant refers to these laws
as Categories, necessary as the laws of logic are, and recognized
by the pure understanding as such. The pure understanding, like
the *a priori* imagination, is common to all rational creatures,
indeed it is what constitutes their rationality. The categories enable us, within the framework they supply, to claim knowledge,
which is both of the world of appearances and yet is true *a
priori*, independent of any actual experience. But we would not
be able to apply these laws to the appearances, that is to our
actual moment by moment experience, were it not for two conditions. One is that we can somehow grasp the sense impressions
we have in a way that makes us experience them as fit to fall
into the categories(such as that of cause and effect) which we
possess, ready prepared for them by the pure understanding. The
second is that, in doing this, we ourselves are the steady and
continuing base from which such perceptions and rule-
applications are made. Though the laws we use are common to
everyone, necessarily, yet each one applies them for himself.

The first of these conditions is what Kant refers to as the
Schematism, and is a function of the imagination. In the second
edition of the *Critique* (B181) (*Immanuel Kant's Critique of
Pure Reason* tr. Norman Kemp Smith, Macmillan, 1953, p. 183)
he says 'This schematism of the understanding (which is the
same as imagination) in its application to appearances and their
form is an art concealed in the depth of the human soul whose
real modes of activity Nature is hardly likely ever to allow us
to discover and to have open to our gaze'. Kant may here be
thought to be almost as pessimistic as Hume about really
understanding how we come to be able to move from the inner
world of sense to the outer world of science. It is only in so far
as we can interpret our sense experience that we can make this

move; and it is plain that, like Hume, he gives this crucial interpretative task to the imagination.

But the second condition of knowledge, that there should be for each of us a continuous point of view, a self which is the individual constructer of what is nevertheless a common universe is perhaps of even greater significance, and is new. For Hume, the idea of a 'self' had been as fragmented as the idea of the external world. All he could claim to be aware of was a series or 'bundle' of perceptions, with no recognizable 'owner'. Kant introduced the notion of an observer. Without this idea of 'myself as observer', even though it has no content (that is, it tells us nothing about 'myself' except that I am an observer), there would still be no way of finally settling the question whether all my thoughts and beliefs about the external world were not in fact thoughts and beliefs about my own imaginings. But if it is the case that my perceptions of the external world come to me, as Kant argued, from a particular spatial and temporal point of view, to a 'me' who is firmly situated in the phenomenal world, then the externality of the world is assured. One cannot make sense of the idea of an external world unless there is an observer, looking out at it. But once the concept of the observer is introduced, an object to be observed comes with it.

In this respect, then, Kant advanced on Hume. He made our ordinary peasant-like assumptions about the world out there, waiting to be perceived and known, seem better founded. The invisible 'I', the 'I' who perceives, is fitted out *a priori* with the imagination (as well as the necessary categories of the understanding) which allows me to interpret the world of nature. If there is no 'I' there is no inner world. But then there is no outer world either. The two must stand in contrast to each other; if one exists, so does the other. Though the world of nature, according to Kant, is still the world 'as it appears', we can claim to know it, and to understand it according to laws applicable to it by every rational creature. The mystery of how on earth we manage to communicate with each other has been solved. For the world as it appears is genuinely common to us all, though grasped and understood by each.

Kant argued, and sought to prove, that we are committed to understanding the world that appears to us through the senses as consisting of objects separate from ourselves. The categories of the pure understanding are, he held, responsible for ordering and rendering intelligible the spatio-temporal world of appearances with which we are acquainted by intuition. And these categories are imposed by us, from within, and yet are necessarily the same for every creature possessed of reason. The so-called Copernican Revolution of the *Critique of Pure Reason* was indeed revolutionary. Kant had argued that we can know about the external world, that science and general truth are possible, because the framework through which our knowledge is channelled is supplied from ourselves. And for all of us, being rational, the framework of thought is the same. Moreover, the relation between the inner and the outer is given, once and for all, in our experience itself. He could have said, and did indeed imply, that language and the use of language entail that such an 'objective' world exists, as well as the 'subjective' inner world. It had been an impossible problem for the empiricists (and it would have been for Descartes had he considered it) to account for the fact that we can successfully communicate with one another. For if all we have is inner experience (even if by good fortune we are possessed of imagination to make it seem outer), it must be impossible for language ever to get started. Each, if we used signs or words at all, would be referring only to himself. Locke especially recognized this difficulty. He says

> Though words as they are used by men can properly... signify nothing but the ideas that are in the mind of the speaker, yet they in their thoughts give them secret reference to two other things. First, they suppose their words to be marks of the ideas in the minds also of other men with whom they communicate. Secondly because men would not be thought to talk barely of their own imaginings but of things as really they are, therefore they suppose their words to stand also for the reality of things. (John Locke, *Essay Concerning Human Understanding* Bk III, ch. 2, ed. A. S. Pringle-Pattison, Clarendon Press, 1928, p. 225).

Locke thus supposes that people secretly make language work by supposing it to refer to shared experiences and to the outside world. But he does not tell us what entitles people to make these hidden hypotheses, or why they make them, except to avoid seeming too egocentric or fanciful. Above all he does not tell us how it comes about that these hypotheses work so well.

But of course language users are perfectly entitled to refer their words to the world outside themselves; nor need they make any secret of it. Kant's Copernican Revolution was designed to ensure this result.

The revolution in philosophy that has come about in this century (a revolution just as potent as Kant's, and foreshadowed in his *Critique*) is the recognition that the question how language can be made to refer to the public world, as well as to the private, inner world of 'ideas' need never be asked again. It was the wrong question all along. This was the revolution brought about by Ludwig Wittgenstein (1889–1951) in his later work, especially in the *Philosophical Investigations* (Blackwell, 1968).

According to Wittgenstein language was meant in its first origins to apply publicly, to the shared external world. This seems obvious enough now. But to a Cartesian it would seem astonishing and counter-intuitive to say that the command 'Feed the cat' is a more direct and fundamental use of language than 'I have a pain' or 'I feel sad'. From where we stand now it seems plain that words are essentially, not merely derivatively, concerned with a public world, about which we need to communicate, and in which we need to act and get others to act. Descartes, however, was committed to the view that we know the contents of our own minds better than we know anything else (see his *Meditation* II in *The Philosophical Works*, vol. I, p. 157) and he would have held, therefore, had he thought about it, that our words must refer primarily to these contents. Our own ideas are all we have.

The fact is, of course, that besides ourselves and whatever things there may be in the world, there are also other people. Descartes believed that if we refer to other people's ideas or feelings, we can do so only by analogy with ourselves. But this is not the way language works. An important and highly complex function of language is its use to communicate what may be called 'states of mind'; and with this Descartes would have agreed. What he would have found hard to accept is the assertion that when I describe someone else's state of mind, stating, for example, that he is angry or afraid, I am using the words in exactly the same way as I use them when I refer to myself. There is no need to suppose that I am using them in a sense given merely by analogy. If the words I use did not mean the same whether I am speaking of myself or of another, there would be no possibility of interpersonal communication about states of mind. And this, happily, is not the case.

In his book *Individuals: An Essay in Descriptive Metphysics* (Anchor Books, 1963) P. F. Strawson argues for this position. He starts from the proposition that a 'person' is what he calls a Primitive Concept, that is, one that we can neither dispense with nor sub-divide. A person is an object that we are aware of in the world, possessed of various characteristics which we ascribe to him as predicates, in language. Strawson distinguishes all predicates into M predicates, such as we apply to all physical objects, including persons; and P predicates, which are all the other predicates that we apply to persons. For example, 'weighing ten stone' is an M predicate, 'being patriotic' or 'feeling anxious' are P predicates. His argument is that we could never apply a P predicate to anyone other than ourselves, if we could not apply M predicates as well as P predicates to others, and apply both to the very same indivisible individual person, the indissoluble primitive object of awareness. We have to be able to hear, see, weigh, knock into persons, that is, perceive in various ways their physical characteristics, if we are to be able to assign to them a point of view, that is, a capacity to see and react to the world in different ways, and thus be properly described by P predicates. While accepting Strawson's distinction between kinds of predicate, and his insistence that what we perceive and apply these predicate to in our language is one and the same individual object, I would prefer not to introduce the word 'person' as the generic name of this object. I regard the word 'person', to borrow the words of John Locke, as 'a forensic term' (*Essay*, Bk II, ch. 27, p. 198). That is to say that whether or not to deem someone to be a person may be a matter of decision, even of dispute. The term is at least sometimes used in association with such legal concepts as the ownership of property, competence to make decisions and so on. It is therefore, in my view, an unsuitable term to designate a basic particular, instantly perceived as such. I believe that the true basic particular is an individual member of the human species.

I concede that there may be difficulties in my preferred use, for there are known to exist members of the human species to whom we cannot at a particular time, or in particular circumstances, apply any P predicates at all, such as those who are in a coma or a persistent vegitative state, or who are embryos fertilized in a dish in the laboratory. These Strawson would say are not 'persons', and therefore are not, presumably, basic particulars, though human and alive. However I believe that it is important to signify, by our designation, that what makes these basic particulars indispensable and indissoluble as items of our experience is that they are, as we are, human animals. That some of these animals are damaged or exceedingly immature can be accommodated as forming a class of exceptions. Their humanity is not in doubt, though how we treat them in the practical world may be disputed. In any case, however we may wish to designate these objects of our awareness, the point is the same: wherever a P predicate is appropriate, we recognize that we are applying it to the very same object as that to which certain M predicates are applicable; moreover, these P predicates mean the same whether they are applied to one of these objects or to me myself.

To say that P predicates mean the same whether they are applied by me to myself, or by me to others, is not necessarily, or usually, to say that how it comes about that we apply such predicates has to be the same in each case. I may simply know, without specially observing it, that I am feeling sad today. Often, for some identifiable reason, sadness infects all my thoughts and perceptions, so that I cannot be unaware of it; sometimes the feeling is apparent without my having thought of the cause, for which I may have to search; often the cause and the feeling are both manifest to me. On the other hand, of someone else, I may say 'he is sad' first and foremost because I see the way his shoulders droop, or I see him brushing away a tear. But it is only because 'sadness' has the very same sense whether I ascribe it to myself or to him that, when he comes to talk to me, I understand his sadness. To quote Strawson,

> It is essential to the character of P predicates that they have both first and third person ascriptive use, that they are both self-ascribable otherwise than on the basis of observation of

behaviour, and other-ascribable on the basis of behaviour criteria. To learn their use is to learn both aspects of their use.
In order to have this type of concept, one must both be a
self-ascriber of such predicates, and must see every other as a
self-ascriber. (*Individuals*, p. 108).

Now this category of predicates has manifestly not been
simply invented by Strawson, even though his way of delineating
them is new. The fact is that we understand them and use them
every day. So if our language embraces both our own feelings
(to use a shorthand expression) and those of others by the use
of the very same words, it is easy to see how we may claim to
understand someone who says, for example, that he is sad. To
go one step further than this, not only to understand him but
to sympathize with him, requires the plainly imaginative step
of adopting his point of view, which is other than our own.
Because he is, and is immediately seen by us to be, a member
of the human species, as we are, we know that, both literally
and metaphorically, he has a point of view, and that his point
of view is his own, not ours. But it is the precise function of
imagination to enable us to consider that which is not the case;
and we can therefore consider how it would be with us, how
things would look, if we saw things not through our own eyes
but through his. And so I can properly claim to know what
he feels, and feel it as well, though doubtless less intensely.

Sympathy, then, is a function of imagination. It functions
because we recognize others as members of the species of which
we are members. I do not wish to deny that we are, to a limited
extent, capable of sympathy with other animals, when we recognize in them something we believe to be shared between
species, such as pain, fear, anxiety, hunger or thirst. In such
cases we may confidently claim to know what lies behind the
behaviour of the animals. But if we go further, and claim to feel
exactly what they feel, there is quite self-evidently a danger of
anthropomorphism.

Referring to sympathy, Hume puts it thus:

The minds of all men are similar in their feelings and operations, nor can anyone be actuated by any affection of which all
others are not in some degree susceptible. As in strings equally

wound up, the motion of one communicates itself to the rest;
so all the affections readily pass from one person to another,
and beget correspondent movements in every human creature.
(*Treatise* Bk III, pt III, sec. I, p. 575)

Earlier in the *Treatise* (Bk II, pt I, sec. XI, p. 317) Hume wrote
'No quality of human nature is more remarkable, both in itself
and in its consequences than that propensity we have to sympathize with others and to receive by communication their
inclinations and sentiments'. Let us suppose that we come upon
a man who is in pain. We have, in Hume's terminology, certain
impressions. We see his facial expression, we hear his groans.
Imagination has, among its powers, the power, as we have seen,
to create ideas out of present impressions. And, when we encounter this man, as we are not suffering pain ourselves, it
might be thought that we would have only the idea of his pain.
But very powerful imagination can not only make ideas out of
impressions; it can also present ideas so strongly to us as to
make them, in turn, into impressions. Poets and orators, imaginative geniuses, can do this. They can present us with ideas
in so forceful a manner as to make us feel, or see that which
they describe. After all there is no absolute difference in kind
between ideas and impressions. Both, according to Hume, are
mental experiences, experienced in ourselves. The only difference
lies in their relative force or vivacity. And so, because we are
in many ways so like the man in pain, being also human, and
disliking and suffering from the kinds of things he dislikes and
suffers from, although all we actually experience is the outer
signs of his pain, yet we can, by imagination, produce so
powerful an idea of pain as to be almost an impression of pain
itself. This is still more obviously true if we think of seeing
someone who is amused, or elated, or in great sorrow. Here we
may actually share his amusement, elation or sorrow. Imagination allows us to feel what he feels, turning mere ideas into
impressions, competent to do so because of the similarity between us. The closer we are (literally and metaphorically) to the
sufferer, the more strongly our imagination works. This, Hume
says (*Treatise* p. 319) is the nature and cause of sympathy; and
'tis after this manner we enter so deep into the opinions and
affections of others.'

There is, then, a strong philosophical tradition which gives to imagination the task of allowing us access not only to the natural, external world as a whole, but also to the minds and thoughts and feelings of other people. So if Hume had been prepared (as in some moods he almost was) to admit the validity of imagination as a way of knowing, he would have been able to accept more readily than he did our position in the world. We are separate, certainly, each with his own point of view, but we are not irrevocably shut up in our own bodies, peering out onto the world (including the world of other people) whose real existence remains problematic. That we are not in fact so boxed in is shown by the existence and the efficacy of language.

We may fairly claim, then, that imagination can dissolve what had seemed to Descartes and his successors the insoluble problem of the relation between the inner and the outer, the mental and the corporeal. Human beings are capable of grasping and understanding the world of which they form a part. They are observers, but not observers made of wholly different stuff. Their existence is in space and time, alongside all material objects, and alongside other humans.

2

Imagination and the Idea
of Genius

In this chapter I shall explore some features of the Romantic imagination, that is the imagination both deployed and discussed at the transition from the eighteenth to the nineteenth century. I shall consider it as it bears on the relation between the inner and the outer world, between the 'I', and his understanding and recognition of truth. To explore this will be to bring out the tension between two beliefs. The first belief is that imagination and truth are diametrically opposed to one another, the one personal, unreliable and fleeting, the other shared, timeless and enduring. This may be called the objective or scientific view of truth. The opposite belief is that there is no such thing as a truth about the world that is not mediated, grasped and understood by the imagination of the individual. This is the belief that lies behind Abram's metaphor of the lamp (see pp. 1–2). It is incorporated in its purest form in John Keats' letter to Benjamin Bailey: 'I am certain of nothing but the holiness of the Heart's affections and the Truth of Imagination... The imagination may be compared to Adam's dream – he awoke and found it truth' (*The Letters of Keats, 1814-21*, ed. H. E. Rollins, Harvard University Press, vol. 1, Letter 43, pp. 183–7). The persuasiveness of the second of these ideas dominated the Romantic consciousness, and is nowadays so universally accepted that we are in danger of being overwhelmed. It may be agreed that we cannot go back to the image of the mirror. But the danger of the lamp image is that each of us may seem separately to have a lamp of our own; or at least it may be held that groups of us share a lamp: women have one lamp, men another, scientists one, historians another; for every group, its own imagination, and its own discourse.

Such relativism seems to me not only destructive, but, as I shall argue, based on false ideas of the relation that actually exists between humans, and between humans and the rest of the world. However, to pursue this argument it is necessary first to consider the origins of the belief in such a personalized universe.

There were philosophical influences that worked on many of the Romantic writers, not least the influence of Kant and his German successors. We have seen how Kant made it possible to claim genuine knowledge of an external world of things as they appeared in space and time, and how this possibility depended, according to his critical philosophy, on the power of the imagination that was, mysteriously, common to everyone, the given, *a priori* imagination. Coleridge, that true prophet of the Romantic age, described how Kant's *Critique* took possession of him, 'as with a giant's hand' (Samuel Taylor Coleridge, *Biographia Literaria*, Fenners, 1817; reprinted by The Scolar Press, 1971, ch. IX, p. 145.) Yet there were other influences on him as well, going further back. In the same chapter of the *Biographia*, Coleridge speaks of 'studying in the school of Locke, Berkeley, Leibniz and Hartley', and finding none of them satisfying. But we should not forget that in letters written in 1796 and 1797, the first to Thelwall, the second to Southey (Coleridge, *Collected Letters*, ed. Griggs, OUP 1956), Coleridge referred to himself as a Berkeleian; and his second son was named Berkeley after the philosopher. There is no doubt that idealism, as propounded by Berkeley, was in the air, and that Coleridge was not immune to its influence.

Berkeley's *Principles of Human Knowledge* was published in 1710, and was praised by Hume, though hardly mentioned by Kant. In it, Berkeley proposed to solve the Cartesian problem of the relation between the inner and the outer world by asserting that the world consisted of nothing but spirits (or minds) and their ideas. This doctrine (or dogma: Berkeley produced very little in the way of argument to justify it) was generally seen, both by philosophers and by ordinary people, to reduce the world to nothing but dreams or fantasies. Berkeley himself, however, insisted that it was a way of returning people to common sense. For it enabled them to give up the belief that there was some mysterious physical substance, separate from themselves, with which they could never be directly acquainted, but whose properties were nevertheless conveyed to them through the senses. Such a belief, he argued, was strictly non-sensical. All we can know or experience are ideas. And since everyone would agree that ideas exist only if there is a mind or spirit to 'have' them, so what we call things, being collections of ideas, must exist only in so far as they are 'had' or experienced by a mind. The existence of things consists in their being perceived by somebody. What we refer to as the outer world is nothing but consistent and regular sets of ideas usually experienced one with another. All this Berkeley regards as totally self-evident:

> Some truths there are so near and obvious to the mind, that a man need only open his eyes to see them. Such I take this important one to be, to wit, that all the choir of heaven and furniture of the earth, in a word all those bodies which compose the mighty frame of the world, have not any subsistence without a mind, that their being is to be perceived or known; that consequently as long as they are not actually perceived by me, or do not exist in my mind or that of any other created spirit, they must either have no existence at all, or else subsist in the mind of some eternal spirit: it being perfectly unintelligible... to attribute to any single part of them an existence independent of spirit. (*Principles of Human Knowledge* Pt 1, para. VI, Everyman ed., 1954, p. 115)

This is a statement of ontological belief, backed up by the implication that to believe anything else would be an absurd paradox. It constitutes a vision of reality, though apparently deduced from self-evident premises. A part of the vision, and one on which Berkeley insisted, was that God's existence is essential to our understanding of the world, and our ability to feel at home in it. For if it were not that God shared his ideas with us, our ideas would display no regularity or predictability. When we expect that heat will make water boil, for example, we are relying not on any actual power in the heat to produce an effect, but on the active will of God, to bring it about that we experience first heat and then the bubbling water. He could choose to make things happen otherwise, but he does not. If the world seems to be a unified and coherent system, that is because it displays the consistent workings of God's mind.

This vision of the world as spirit and the ideas of spirit was attractive in two ways. In the first place it provided philosophical backing for the picture of nature as a book, in which we could read the language of God. In seeking to understand nature, we are seeking to know God. Secondly, in seeking knowledge, any knowledge, we are coming to know ourselves. For whatever we come to know, it is the content of our own minds which is the sole object of knowledge. Self-understanding and the understanding of nature are therefore one and the same.

The first of these pictures produced a great stock of imagery: 'Surely nature is a book, and every page rich with sacred hints. To an attentive mind the garden turns preacher, and its blooming tenants are so many lively sermons' (James Hervey, *Reflections on a Flower Garden*, in *Meditations and Contemplations*, 1746). Such a vision justified and explained the passionate pursuit of accurate and detailed nature study, such as that of Gilbert White, and many other naturalists. Coleridge speaks of his debt to such Enthusiasts or mystics:

> The writings of these mystics... contributed to keep alive the heart in the head; gave me an indistinct, yet stirring and working presentiment, that all the products of the mere reflective faculty took part in DEATH, and were as the rattling twigs and sprays in winter, into which a sap was yet to be propelled, from some root to which I had not yet penetrated. (*Biographia Literaria* ch. IX, vol. 1, p. 144)

Coleridge admitted, in particular, to the influence of William Law, a thorough Platonist. Law spoke of 'Temporal nature, opened to us by the spirit of God, which becomes a volume of holy instruction and leads us into all the mysteries and secrets of eternity', and he went on 'For as everything in temporal nature is descended out of that which is eternal and stands as a palpable and visible outbirth of it, so when we know how to separate the grossness, death and darkness of time from it, we find what it is in its eternal state'. (Quoted in Isaac Walton, *Notes and Materials for an adequate biography of William Law*.) For Law, nature speaks of eternity.

The second strand, the thought that the pursuit of knowledge is the pursuit of self-knowledge, was part of the non-
philosophical legacy of Kant, who introduced the notion of
the 'I' whose point of view unified the world of experience.
Of course Kant's writings were less than perfectly understood.
But it is often only the crudest or the most exaggerated accounts
of what philosophers actually write that are ever taken up into
the general consciousness, to become part of the spirit of the
age. Their influence may be nevertheless pervasive.

In one way the solitary exploring Romantic figure, remotely
Kantian in origin, was more bleak than the searcher after the
mind of the Almighty. He was out on his own, with no cosy
support in his quests. And his solitude led him to despair. But
there was, of course, something grand and heroic about the
solitary traveller, the Child Harold figure of Romanticism. 'Are
not the mountains, waves, and skies, a part/Of me and of my
soul, as I of them?' (*Byron: Poetical Works*, ed. Frederick Page,
corr. John Jump, OUP, 1970, p. 220). The sentiment of the
grand connections between humans and the universe was a
new field in which the Romantic imagination seemed to have
free play.

The connections were partly, it was hoped, to issue in knowledge and understanding. At the end of the eighteenth century
people deeply wanted to understand; and understanding was,
and is, unlike common or shared knowledge, necessarily in some
sense personal. It is the attribute of an individual 'I'. When he
claims to have reached understanding, it is he, that individual,
who possesses something within his grasp. What he *has* is an
interpretation which fits with what he already has: his new
understanding adds to his possessions.

The growth of new scientific knowledge, and thus the search
for understanding in the fields of physics, chemistry, optics or
medicine went along with new ways of writing and painting, and
the same people sometimes took part with equal enthusiasm
both in what we should call scientific activities, and in the
creative and artistic. It was held that the external world would
reveal its secrets, if looked at clearly and directly. And this
careful looking was seen to be, perhaps, a revelation of the
mind of the creator, but certainly an exercise of the individual
observer's imagination. What was received from nature was an

image, an idea which could be kept alive, perpetuated and shared only if imaginatively grasped. It was at this point that the concept of an individual observer as a *genius* became relevant. The greater the genius of the individual, the more readily could he produce a vision of the natural world, new, yet acceptable to all. Sometimes the reliance on genius, or originality, was deplored; but it was seen to be inevitable. Edward Young put it thus:

> An Original may be said to be of a vegetable nature; it rises spontaneously from the vital root of genius; it grows, it is not made: imitations are often a sort of manufacture wrought up by those mechanics, art and labour, out of pre-existent materials not their own... We read imitation with somewhat of his languor who listens to a twice-told tale: our spirits rouze at an original; that is a perfect stranger, and all throng to learn news from a foreign land: and though it comes, like an Indian prince, adorned with feathers only, having little of weight; yet of our attention it will rob the more solid if not equally new. Thus every telescope is lifted at a new-discovered star; it makes a hundred astronomers in a moment, and denies equal notice to the sun. (Edward Young, *Conjectures on Original Composition*, 1759)

Yet, though originality and the search after novelty might sometimes seem frivolous, the notion that there was such a thing as genius, imaginative creativity beyond the norm, became an increasing part of the Romantic stock-in-trade of the late eighteenth century. Johnson did not notice this sense of the word 'genius' in his dictionary. Before the eighteenth century the word had designated either the particular spirit (personified or not) of a place, or, when used of people, their particular bent or cast of mind. Yet Hume defined it clearly at the beginning of the *Treatise* (Bk I, Pt I, sec. VII, p. 24):

> Nothing is more admirable, than the readiness, with which the imagination suggests its ideas, and presents them at the very instant, in which they become necessary or useful. The fancy runns from one end of the universe to the other in collecting those ideas, which belong to any subject. One would think the whole intellectual world of ideas was at once subjected to our view, and that we did nothing but pick out such as were most

proper for our purpose. There may not, however, be any present, beside those very ideas that are thus collected by a kind of magical faculty of the soul, which, tho' it be always most perfect in the greatest geniuses, and is properly what we call a genius, is however inexplicable by the utmost efforts of the human understanding.

Kant explored the notion of genius further, in the *Critique of Judgement* (1790). Indeed from this point, the cult of genius became part of the German literary scene, associated especially with *Sturm und Drang*. The idea of genius was often closely connected with the idea, seen already in the writings of William Law, that nature reveals eternity to creatures who are themselves temporal. The distinction between the beautiful and the sublime, part of the stock-in-trade of the aesthetic theory of the late eighteenth and early nineteenth centuries, incorporated the same idea, and the distinction was central to Kant's theory. Beauty was held, for example by Home (whose book, *Elements of Criticism*, published in London in 1760, was translated into German and certainly read by Kant) to be a matter of rules, the following of which produced order, symmetry and harmony. In contrast, sublimity, which was discussed by, among others, Addison and Burke, had to be distinguished from beauty because the very means by which it seemed to excite pleasurable reactions, its vastness, wildness and lack of order were the precise opposite of the limited and constrained orderliness held to be the marks of beauty. Kant drew the distinction thus:

> Natural beauty conveys a finality in its form, making the object appear as it were preadapted to our judgement, so that it thus forms of itself an object of delight. That which, on the other hand, in our apprehension of it excites the feeling of the sublime may appear in point of form to contravene the ends of our power of judgement, to be ill-shaped to our faculty of presentation, and to be as it were an outrage on the imagination, and yet is judged all the more sublime on that account. (*Critique of Judgement*, trans. Meredith, OUP, 1952, p. 91)

Kant is suggesting that when we hold a thing to be beautiful, we can in some way immediately grasp it, and see in it a design or pattern whose sense we understand. When we judge something to be sublime, on the other hand, we are amazed by it. We could in no way have created its sublimity ourselves, by the application of a rule. It is when we recognize sublimity that we create a concept of infinity and of eternity which we recognize as literally beyond us. Kant accepted the current further distinction, contained for example in Hugh Blair's *Lectures on Rhetoric* (1783), between that idea of sublimity which arises from the contemplation of vast numbers and that which arises from the contemplation of vast power. In each case we are confronted with our own inability to frame a sensory image, whether of the numbers or of the power. Yet in each case we recognize, in contrast, something immense about ourselves, that we are able to calculate in terms of these great numbers, though we cannot envisage them; and, in the other case, that we have a quite different power, the power to resist pressure or temptation, for the sake of an ideal, to follow the moral law, though the heavens fall. In Kant's system, it is Reason which gives us these abilities. We experience sublimity, and get pleasure from it, because there is something about human nature, its rationality, which goes beyond the rest of nature. Human weakness in the face of the vast is contrasted with a human strength that is still greater; and it is this truth, a truth about ourselves, which gives us a sense of elation, rather than simple fear or oppression in the face of the sublime. Kant makes the point dramatically:

Bold overhangings and threatening rocks, thunder clouds piled up the vault of heaven, borne along with flashes and peals, volcanoes in all their violence of destruction, hurricanes leaving desolation in their track, the boundless ocean in rebellious force, the high waterfall of some mighty river make our power of resistance of trifling moment in comparison to their might. But ... their aspect is all the more attractive for its fearfulness: and we readily call these objects sublime because they raise the forces of the soul above the height of vulgar commonplace, and discover within us a power ... of quite another kind which gives us courage to be able to measure ourselves against the seeming omnipotence of nature. In the immeasurableness of nature we find our own limitation. But with this we also find...another non-sensuous standard, one which has that infinity itself under it as a unit, and in comparison with which everything in nature is small. (*Critique of Judgment*, p. 110)

The idea embodied in the sublime object is beyond representation or complete explanation, but yet it can be apprehended and recognized by the human mind. According to Kant, the man of genius, as distinct from the man of ordinary imaginative powers, will be the one who, in poetry or painting or music, comes closest to expressing these great ideas of reason which cannot be exactly expressed. The imagination, Kant says, is a powerful agent 'for creating as it were a second nature out of the materials supplied to it by the first nature' (ibid., p. 117). This second nature in some ways surpasses the first, since the images in terms of which it is presented are all attempts to reach beyond the mere appearance of things, to that which lies behind them. The man of genius, Kant says, 'attempts to body forth the idea of reason to sense with a completeness for which nature itself affords no parallel' (ibid.). His representations 'strain after something lying out beyond the confines of sense.' Those ideas which the genius strives to express and to present so that others can grasp, or nearly grasp, them are called by Kant Aesthetic Ideas. An aesthetic idea is a 'representation of the imagination which induces much thought, yet without the possibility of any definite thought whatever, i.e. concept being adequate to it, and which language, consequently, can never get quite on level terms with, or render completely intelligible.' The works of genius, which body forth these ideas are 'exemplary'. Such a work cannot be copied, for it is unique; but it sets a standard for others.

From Kant's time on, imagination was increasingly recognized to be an essential part of making sense of the world, even for those without the elevated powers of genius. Sensation alone, without imagination, was not enough for understanding, whether the understanding of man himself or of the natural world as a whole. This became the orthodoxy of the nineteenth century.

Kant, for his part, distinguished great scientific insights, such as those of Newton, from the genius of great creative artists, on the grounds that deduction from principles lay at the root of scientific discovery, and the process of discovery could therefore be laid bare, whereas the processes of artistic genius were mysterious, and no language could account for the greatness of its outcome. Not everyone agreed with this distinction, at least at the beginning of the nineteenth century. For it could be argued that science, just as much as descriptive writing or landscape painting, depended on observation of nature. So the very same values might seem to attach to science as to art. The pursuit of understanding was common to both. Thus Sir Humphry Davy, writing in *The Director* (no. 19 1807) (*Works of Sir Humphry Davy*, vol. 8, 1840) said

> The contemplation of the laws of the universe is connected with an immediate tranquil exaltation of the mind, and pure mental enjoyment. The perception of truth is almost as simple a feeling as the perception of beauty; and the genius of Newton, of Shakespeare, of Michael Angelo and of Handel are not very remote in character from each other. Imagination, as well as reason, is necessary to perfection in the philosophical mind. A rapidity of combination, a power of perceiving analogies, and of comparing them by facts is the creative source of discovery. Discrimination and delicacy of sensation, so important in physical research, are other words for taste; and the love of nature is the same passion as the love of the magnificent, the sublime and the beautiful.

Imagination used in the interpretation of what is seen and heard is thus as essential to the discovery of truth as of beauty.

Now for Davy, and many of his contemporaries, to say that something was the product of an imaginative genius or even simply of imagination, would not in the least suggest that it was not true. Hume's anxiety about the lowness and frivolity of the imaginative faculty had been left behind. We can see emerging in the late eighteenth and early nineteenth centuries the belief that it is creative imagination alone which enables us to respond to the world, and discover there what is true. And at the same time it seemed plain that this response to nature entailed a new *self*-awareness, an essential part of the imaginative process. The imaginative genius was both self-absorbed, and absorbed in the natural world.

Coleridge wrote explicitly of the contribution of the imagination to our response to nature in his poem *Dejection: an Ode*, written (in one of its many versions) in 1802. This poem is an important source for his theory of how imagination worked in practice. It is concerned with his own feeling of loss; the loss of 'genius'. Having described the spectacle of the stars behind clouds, and the crescent moon, Coleridge says:

> I see them all so excellently fair
> I see, not feel, how beautiful they are.
>
> ...It were a vain endeavour
> Though I should gaze forever
> On that green light that lingers in the West:
> I may not hope from outward forms to win
> The passion and the life whose fountains are within.
>
> O lady, we receive but what we give
> And in our life alone does nature live...
> Ah, from the soul itself must issue forth
> A light, a glory, a fair luminous cloud
> Enveloping the earth.
> And from the soul itself must there be sent
> A sweet and potent voice of its own birth
> Of all sweet sounds the life and element.

Coleridge calls this 'sweet voice', this music of the soul by the name 'joy'. He goes on:

> There was a time when, though my path was rough,
> This joy within me dallied with distress,
> And all misfortunes were but as the stuff
> Whence fancy made me dreams of happiness...
> But now afflictions bow me down to earth.
> Nor care I that they rob me of my mirth,
> But Oh each visitation
> Suspends what nature gave me at my birth
> My shaping spirit of imagination.

Shaping imagination is identified here with 'joy'. The idea of joy is as important in this context as that of genius; indeed they overlap. 'Joy' suggests an inexplicable and mysterious delight, an excitement and satisfaction, and a conviction that the experience is worth having for itself, not for any consequences that it may bring. To 'enjoy' is to delight in something for itself. Joy is therefore a central concept both for aesthetic theory, and for any investigation of the intrinsic satisfactions of understanding. Later, the word was used both by Proust, in his discovery of past time, and by C. S. Lewis in his exploration of moments of insight, his secret 'epiphanies'. According to Coleridge, joy comes from within ourselves: 'We in ourselves delight', he says. Without imagination, we merely see or hear, and even if we see or hear that the objects of the senses are beautiful, we cannot feel that they are so. The difference is this: in feeling the beauty of objects, we enjoy not only the common, shared pleasures of the senses, but also the private pleasures of the imagination, peculiar to ourselves, and such that we have to struggle to articulate them. They lie, Kant said, always just beyond the reach of language. This, in short, is the lesson of the Romantic imagination. When Coleridge thought that the 'shaping spirit of imagination' had deserted him, he thought that thereby he had lost the power to understand the language of nature. The world of nature can speak to us if and only if we can shape it into an idea, or impression, of our own. We may then try, with greater or lesser success, to interpret this language for others than ourselves.

As we have seen, Coleridge, in several letters of this period, declared himself a thoroughgoing Berkeleian. He was perhaps weaned back to a modified dualistic theory of the world only by his reading of Kant, even though he may not have very well understood what he read. At any rate, Kant would have introduced into his world the idea of the observer whose shaping imagination forms the very nature he seeks to read and to interpret.

The idea of an imagination both self-absorbed and constructive of the perceived world was central to Wordsworth as well as to Coleridge. We know that Wordsworth, perhaps with greater passion than Coleridge, had from his boyhood often felt (rather than thought) that there was no world except the world of his own ideas. He says of himself, 'I was often unable to think of external things as having external existence, and I communed with all I saw as something not apart from but inherent in my own immaterial nature.' (Fenwick note to the *Ode: Intimations of Immortality. Notes Dictated to Isabella Fenwick*, 1843.)

Whether Wordsworth or Coleridge or any other poet or painter was actually a follower, even a reader, of Berkeley is not important. What concerns us here is the indisputable fact that idealism was quite familiar, a part of the *Zeitgeist*, and that it led to a quite general erosion of the line between the inner and the outer worlds. Words such as 'form' or 'shape', 'prospect' or 'perception', as well as the word 'idea' itself were all used, especially by Wordsworth, indifferently of the inner and the outer. Perhaps it would be better to say that such words were used as essentially and fruitfully ambiguous, so that the distinction between the inner and the outer could not, and deliberately could not, be made with their help. (For an excellent discussion of this point see C. C. Clarke, *Romantic Paradox: An Essay on the Poetry of Wordsworth*, Routledge & Kegan Paul, 1962.)

Wordsworth thought of the world as, on the one hand, something other than himself, something to be discovered, loved, questioned for what it could reveal: on the other hand, and at the same time, he was convinced that what we perceive is a picture or prospect composed by ourselves, that it is mind-dependent, and that in scanning it and seeking to understand it we shall in the end discover truths that are truths about ourselves, or rather about human nature, as exemplified by ourselves. This ambiguity could be taken to be the central conundrum of Romanticism: is truth inner or outer, personal or scientific, ephemeral or permanent? It was the sudden apparent urgency of such questions as these that brought imagination into the centre of epistemology, and into the search for truth both through the description and observation of the immediately perceived, and through the images of poetry and the visual arts.

Wordsworth, we must conclude, held truth to be both inner and outer. His perceptions, and his reflections on them, led to truths which were, he thought, permanent, and true for all time, and were true of a separate world that was not himself, however much he contributed to its construction. Moreover, his concept of truth incorporated the notion of time in another way. For he held that truth could be reached only through remembered perceptions. What happens to a child is retained, and turned, by the adult he becomes, into a truth that has an application beyond himself. There is a kind of alchemy in memory which turns the ephemeral impression into the eternal verity. The child receives immediate and instantaneous impressions which turn out, when he revisits them, to contain what is timeless. Because memory is at the centre of this process, it follows that the discovery of truth is personal; for it is one continuously existing individual who had the experience and who later revisits it, and turns it into truth. Memory, though a species of imagination, has a validity which imagination in its other manifestations may not be thought necessarily to have. The way to overcome Hume's fears that imagination, the thought of the non-existent or absent, is too flighty, too fanciful, to be the foundation of knowledge is to concentrate on that aspect of it, the memory, which we know to give rise to truth. The individual's persistence through time, the indisputable fact that he is the same person as he was when he first received the impressions he recalls, is the essential element of the truth he discovers, though that truth is not limited in its scope to him alone. There are innumerable passages in Wordsworth's poems where this interdependence of truth and time is explored. I will confine myself to two examples, both very familiar.

The first example is from *Lines written above Tintern Abbey* (1798). Almost all of this poem can be read as an expression of the power of imagination, of the images stored in the mind after their first formation, and overlaid on the new images of a revisit, to give rise to new meanings. The poem is quite obviously 'exemplary', a work of genius in Kant's sense, and is made more powerful in that it uses a recognized older form, the 'revisit' or 'nostalgia' poem, common in the earlier part of the century, a tradition which had no epistemological or moral significance, but in its most characteristic form was purely sentimental. Wordsworth transforms the idiom:

> ...These beauteous forms
> Through a long absence, have not been to me
> As is a landscape to a blind man's eye;
> But oft, in lonely rooms, and 'mid the din
> Of towns and cities I have owed to them,
> In hours of weariness, sensations sweet,
> Felt in the blood and felt along the heart...
>   Therefore am I still
> A lover of the meadows and the woods,
> And mountains; and of all that we behold
> From this green earth; of all the mighty world
> Of eye and ear, both what they half-create,

And what perceive; well-pleased to recognize
In Nature and the language of the sense
The anchor of my purest thoughts...

There can be no doubt that here the imagination, the intellect, the emotions and the actual faculties of sight and hearing come together in a 'reading' of the natural world and the world of landscape to which Wordsworth feels that he belongs. We may look at the poem from a variety of critical standpoints. But what it is, first and foremost, is an assertion or expression of a truth, which though permanent and shared, is also an individual understanding, something sought out and achieved; a triumphant conclusion.

My second example is from the *Ode: Intimations of Immortality from Recollections of early Childhood*. The very title of the poem is an expression of the theme of fleeting time recovered and rendered permanent in memory. The power of the poem, the hold that it has over us, lies not merely in its philosophical content but in its emotional swing towards and away from nostalgic melancholy. The ninth stanza encapsulates the philosophy. What a child experiences, especially when at the time he does not fully understand his 'blank misgivings' or his 'high instincts', becomes the source of 'perpetual benediction'. What the poet is thankful for is

...those first affections,
Those shadowy recollections,
Which, be they what they may,
Are yet the fountain-light of all our day,
Are yet the master-light of all our seeing;
Uphold us, cherish, and have power to make
Our noisy years seem moments in the being
  Of the eternal Silence: truths that wake,
To perish never:
Which neither listlessness, nor mad endeavour.
Nor Man nor Boy,
Nor all that is at enmity with joy,
Can utterly abolish or destroy.
Hence in a season of calm weather
Though inland far we be,
Our souls have sight of that immortal sea

Which brought us hither,
And see the children sport upon the shore,
And hear the mighty waters rolling evermore.

How much are we entitled to generalize from these poems? How universal is the achievement which they record? No one will dispute the fact that Wordsworth and Coleridge, together at the end of the eighteenth century and later separately and differently, sought knowledge and understanding through their imaginative contemplation of the natural world. No one will deny that they held imagination (and that aspect of imagination which is memory) to be the vehicle through which alone such understanding could be reached. However, it would also be agreed that to speak of an imaginative vision of the world may strongly suggest the vision of a unique individual, the world seen and understood from behind his eyes. The post-Kantian orthodoxy suggests that to attend to the world is to be conscious both of the world and of oneself; and that in this attention the sharp boundary between the inner and the outer, the so-called 'subjective' and 'objective' collapses. Yet we may still ask whether truth can possibly be the outcome of such self-generated visions. For truth must be something in principle accessible to all. Knowledge of truth is universal, and can be passed on from one source to another. It cannot, one may argue, result from the exercise of one person's imaginative vision, nor rest on one person's remembered experiences.

Such objections as these are the inevitable consequence of the kind of ambiguity inherent in the concept of the image, the form, which is so conspicuous a feature of Wordsworth's thought. Can we do anything to 'objectify' or validate the notion that, in interpreting the layers of images we have of the natural world, we may discover their actual meanings, that is discover truths about the world and about ourselves and our moral lives? It is possible, obviously, to say 'Wordsworth's way of looking at things appeals to me'; or even 'I have understood what he said'. But we may want more than this. Indeed, we are bound to want more, if we want to claim truth for his view of the significance of images. Even if we believe that we can share another person's visions, we seem to need some validation of them before we can claim that they tell us the truth. After all we can understand, sometimes share, someone else's moods, yet we would not necessarily want to say that the sense of doom which you are experiencing, and which I understand, represents the true way of looking at the world.

Perhaps the notion of mood is not wholly irrelevant, and should be pursued. In one of Ivy Compton Burnett's novels (*The Present and the Past*, Gollanz, 1953, p. 9) the nurse says of one of her charges 'Master Henry has one of his moods', to which the child replies 'Seeing the truth about life is not a mood'. But it may nevertheless be akin to a mood. There is, after all, more than one truth about life, and more than one way of regarding oneself in relation to the rest of the universe. Even Wordsworth may have had, in childhood, his more and his less Berkeleian moods. Some ways of looking seem more inevitable, more illuminating, more valuable and fruitful than others. Some visions may seem explanatory in a way that others do not. I would argue that we cannot identify the value we attach both to imagination, and to the kind of understanding that I am suggesting may flow from it, unless we can find some way to distinguish the fruitful and explanatory visions from the rest. Some of our moods appear to provide insight, that is timeless or permanent truth, in a way that others do not. And it is these moods which people seek to pin down, to preserve and express in words, music and painting. Indeed they may feel that they must do so. They have a positive obligation to make themselves understood to others than themselves.

We are accustomed, then, to drawing a distinction between imaginative visions which seem truthful, and those which, though equally derived from imagination, are to be rejected as merely silly or sentimental. Hume, as I have already remarked, distinguished two different kinds of principles of the imagination, the first permanent, irresistible and universal, the second weak and changeable. It is true that he wanted the first kind primarily to embrace those principles which, as we saw, enable us to construct a solid and predictable world, containing reliably recurrent objects such as our practical life and our language demand. Yet he would not have ruled out the kinds of principle of imagination which make us capable of sympathizing with others, and claiming understanding of what they are thinking or suffering. For, by way of contrast, he offers as an example of the weak and changeable the 'propensity to bestow on external objects the same emotions which human nature observes in itself'. This inclination, he goes on, 'tis true is suppressed by a little reflection, and only takes place in children and poets... It appears in children by their desire of beating the stones which hurt them: in poets by their readiness to personify everything' (*Treatise*, Bk I, Pt IV, sec. 3, p. 224). Hume's poets were pre-Romantic. He, and they, did not know what marvellous powers of moral elevation, what deep revelation of feeling were to be attributed in the future to the world of nature. If he had foreseen this, he might have invented for this weak principle of the imagination the name that Ruskin invented, the Pathetic Fallacy. The question we need to ask is whether it is possible to defend Wordsworth and Coleridge (and many other Romantic poets and artists) against the charge of committing this fallacy, and argue that instead they were legitimately interpreting the natural world, according to a valid, permanent and truthful imaginative insight. After all, the Pathetic Fallacy was named as a fallacy specifically to deal with Wordsworth's supposed imaginative excesses.

Ruskin regarded the ascription of sentiments and sympathies to natural objects as a species of morbidity. He argued that it introduced a 'falseness in all our impressions of external things' (*Modern Painters* iii, ch. 12, 1856). He quoted Wordsworth's description of Peter Bell:

> But nature ne'er could find a way
> Into the heart of Peter Bell.
> In vain, through every changeful year
> Did nature lead him as before;
> A primrose by a river's brim
> A yellow primrose was to him,
> And it was nothing more.

Ruskin's comment was that he preferred the 'very plain and leafy fact of a primrose' to the sentimentality of those for whom the primrose was 'something more', speaking deep thoughts, or symbolizing universal sympathies.

In one of Sir Humphry Davy's early notebooks he wrote:

Today for the first time in my life I have had a distinct sympathy with nature. I was lying on the top of a rock to leeward; the wind was high, and everything in motion; the branches of the oak tree were waving and murmuring to the breeze; yellow clouds, deepened by grey at the base were rapidly floating over the western hills; the yellow stream below was agitated by the breeze; everything was alive, and myself part of the series of visible impressions; I should have felt pain in tearing a leaf from one of the trees.

Hume would not have liked this vision of all-embracing sympathy any more than Ruskin would. He would have argued that sympathy could properly be experienced only between humans, they being in the necessary way understandably similar to each other. Ruskin's objection, on the other hand, would have been based on his implicit assumption that there exist two worlds, the inner and the outer, which can be, and must be, kept distinct. He held that there was some absolutely plain and unambiguous method of describing facts, which in no way intermingled human interpretation with the natural world, nor projected any emotion onto what we see and hear. He wrote: 'The greatest thing a human soul ever does in this world is to see something and tell what it saw in a plain way. To see clearly is poetry, prophecy and religion – all in one' (quoted in J. D. Rosenberg, *The Darkening Glass*, Routledge, 1963, p. 20). What is seen must not be supposed to mean anything other than itself. However, if we read Ruskin's own descriptions (for example of the Alps), the language of which seems to our ear impossibly flowery, we can see that, though he may not suggest that birds or rocks have feelings, yet every adjective and every simile that he employs is emotionally charged to the highest degree. The primrose is by no means only a primrose, it is an object which he looks at with the eye of an impassioned literary man, with a wish to pin it down in his own literary language so that we can see it not as a naked fact, but clothed in his chosen imagery. The idea of the primrose, even for him, is an idea of imagination, an idea with aesthetic significance, and thus, whether he likes it or not, expressive. Ruskin's mistake was to suppose that a sharp line might be drawn between the 'plain descriptive' use of language, and the 'expressive' or 'emotive';

between an engagement with what is *there*, the outer, and what is not there, the inner or imagined. If such a sharp line could indeed be drawn it would be an easy task to distinguish between what is true and what is false, or merely imagined. But things are more complex than that. John Clare wrote: 'I found the poems in the fields/And only wrote them down' (*Sighing for Retirement*, in *Poems of John Clare*, ed. J. W. Tibble, J. M. Dent, 1935, vol. 2, p. 383). The problem is to discover where, in the process of 'finding' and 'writing down', imagination may creep in, and understanding and truth may emerge.

We may see Ruskin as having sought a criterion by which to distinguish what is true from what is fanciful or sentimental, in the pejorative sense. The use of the word 'fallacy' suggests that he thought his criterion could be used precisely; for a fallacy is a logical error, one that can be demonstrated to be erroneous. A different attempt to find such a criterion is at least part of the purpose of Coleridge's distinction between Imagination and Fancy. The passages of *Biographia Literaria* where the distinction is made are notoriously difficult to interpret; and it is certain that a number of different distinctions are being drawn, some of them philosophical, some entirely stylistic. There can, nevertheless, be found there at least a partial move towards the distinction with which Hume was also concerned, between reliable imaginative principles that may give rise to truth, and those that are weak and changeable (see *Biographia Literaria*, vol. 1, ch. XIII, p. 295).

Coleridge divides imagination itself into the primary and the secondary. Primary imagination is that which we deploy in all perception, by which in some inexplicable manner we create the real world, with which we are familiar. Without it the world of sense would be unintelligible and indeed uninhabitable. Primary imagination thus corresponds to the imagination in Hume's epistemology, about which he somewhat tentatively speaks of necessary principles. More directly, it is derived from Kant's *a priori* imagination, that capacity which, apart from any actual experience, provides the means by which our concepts can apply to the world that is given us in experience. It is common to all of us; one person is not, in this sense of 'imagination', more imaginative than another.

Secondary imagination is, Coleridge says, 'an echo' of primary. It, unlike the primary, 'coexists with the conscious will'. 'It dissolves, diffuses, dissipates, in order to recreate.' It is the imagination at work in great works of art. We are taken back, here, to Kant's genius, who strives, never with total success, for the expression of Aesthetic Ideas. Such imagination is essentially creative and vital. This was the power the loss of which Coleridge lamented in the *Ode: Dejection* (see p. 32).

In *Biographia Literaria* (vol. 2, ch. XIV, p. 11) Coleridge makes it plain that secondary imagination is no less inexplicable than primary. He refers to it as 'that synthetic and magical power'. For, though primary and secondary imagination can be distinguished, yet they operate in fundamentally the same way, the one 'making' the world in which we normally lead our lives, the other 'making' new worlds. Fancy, on the other hand is, according to Coleridge, 'no other than a form of memory emancipated from the order of time and space; and blended with, and modified by that empirical phenomenon of the will which we express by the word CHOICE.'

Coleridge would not have denied that memory itself depends upon, indeed is hardly distinguishable from, imagination in the primary sense, for all perceptions, past and present, are so dependent. His interest, however, is centred on the difference between fancy and the secondary imagination. He illustrates the difference, both in *Biographia Literaria* and in numerous essays, especially of Shakespearean criticism, by analysis of actual poems, and imagery in poems. In this criticism, he sought to distinguish the self-consciousness of fancy from the spontaneity and apparent inevitability of imagination. But it is from the passage of the *Biographia* where he describes his first impressions of Wordsworth that we can learn most about what he thought imagination actually was. And this will bring us back to the idea of genius.

In Chapter IV of the *Biographia* (vol. 1, p. 83–92), having praised Wordsworth's style, and remarked on how deeply it impressed him when he heard him read some of his poems, he goes on:

It was not, however, the freedom from false taste... which made so unusual an impression on my feelings immediately,

and subsequently on my judgement. It was the union of deep
feeling with profound thought; the fine balance of truth in observing with the imaginative faculty in modifying the objects
observed; and above all the original gift of spreading the tone,
the atmosphere, and with it the depth and height of the ideal
world around forms, incidents and situations, of which, for the
common view, custom had bedimmed all the luster, had dried
up the sparkle and the dew-drops.

Coleridge went on, in the same passage, to quote something he
had written earlier in *The Friend*:

It [is] the prime merit of genius and its most unequivocal mode
of manifestation, so to represent familiar objects as to awaken
in the minds of others a kindred feeling concerning them and
that freshness of sensation which is the constant accompani-
ment of mental no less than of bodily convalescence... Truths
of all others the most awful and mysterious, yet being at the
same time of universal interest, are too often considered as so
true that they lose all the life and efficacy of truth, and lie
bed-ridden in the dormitory of the soul, side by side, with the
most despised and exploded errors.

It was the life, and the galvanizing property of such genius,
that made Coleridge first decide that imagination, the attribute
of genius, must be something wholly separate from fancy. Of
a poet of genius he says 'You feel him to be a poet inasmuch
as for a time he has made you one, an active creative being'
(p. 85).

The criterion for recognizing imaginings which reveal truth,
rather than those that are merely fanciful, then, seems to rest
on an immediate recognition of genius, where other people
besides the poet or artist himself can, at least momentarily,
be led also to become creative, their imagination, their understanding and their feelings stirred by his, and echoing them.
This is what seems to justify a truth-claim, or at least an insight-
claim, for the imagination. Hume, just as much as Kant and
Coleridge, had recourse to the word 'genius' in his elucidation
of high imaginative powers. The word may seem a cheat, a
non-explanatory cop-out. There is an element of circularity in
employing it to explain what is meant by imagination, since

we could not define the idea itself without reference to imagination in the definition. Yet there is a certain recognizable rightness in this use of the term, even if it is circular. We reserve the word 'genius', otherwise unexplained, for just those people who, as if by magic, seem to widen and deepen our own understanding. We would claim that the person of imaginative genius has access to the truth precisely on the grounds that what he communicates has universality. But the truth conveyed by works of genius cannot simply be accepted. It needs to be grasped by an effort of our own. The original vision has to become our vision. It is this shared creativity of the imagination to which Coleridge refers that seems to validate its claim to be a discoverer and a purveyor of timeless and quite general truth.

3

Imaginative Interpretations

In *The Principles of Art* the philosopher R. G. Collingwood said this:

> The proper meaning of a word (I speak not of technical terms, which kindly godparents furnish soon after birth with neat and tidy definitions, but of words in a living language) is never something on which the word sits perched like a gull on a stone; it is something over which the word hovers like a gull over a ship's stern. (R. G. Collingwood *The Principles of Art*, OUP, 1938, p. 7).

Collingwood has in mind here the definition of fine art; but his image is peculiarly applicable to the word 'imagination' which hovers over the moving history of epistemology and taste. Collingwood goes on to say 'the way to discover the proper meaning is to ask not "what do we mean?" but "what are we trying to mean?"' He proceeds, with perhaps more dogmatism than his hovering gull image should license, to give an account of art which involves a concept of imagination, and its role both in perception and in understanding, which may be thought to be some kind of last-gasp Berkeleian idealism. Attaching labels to types of theory is, however, unprofitable; and Collingwood's view of the function of the imagination in the understanding of art may serve as a bridge between the Romantic theories that were the subject of the last chapter, and those twentieth-century developments that are the main subject of this chapter. If what he says has truth in explaining our interpretation of works of art, it must throw light also on perception in general. It certainly appears to have wider application than to art alone.

In attempting to pin down the function of imagination in perception, Collingwood distinguishes sensation (mere sensation) from attention, awareness or consciousness:

> What we hear... is merely sound. What we attend to is two things at once: a sound, and our act of hearing it. The act of sensation is not present to itself, but it is present, together with its own sensum to the act of attention... Colour, or anger which is no longer seen or felt but attended to, is still colour or anger. When we become conscious of it, it is still the very same colour or anger. But the total experience of seeing or feeling it has undergone change, and in that change, what we see or feel is correspondingly changed. (ibid., p. 206)

Collingwood argues that the crude sensum, or impression, which is essentially fleeting when not attended to, is converted by attention into an idea, and an idea is something which can be kept in existence, as it were visited and revisited and savoured, by imagination. He concludes (p. 215): 'Imagination is the new form which feeling takes when transformed by the activity of consciousness... It is not sensa as such that provide the data for intellect, it is sensa transformed into ideas of imagination.' When we accept something to be a work of art, then, what we accept is an idea; for in attending to it, listening to it or looking at it we have transformed it into an idea. It follows that, in Collingwood's words, 'a tune is an imaginary thing' (ibid., p. 139):

> We all know perfectly well... that a person who hears the noises the instruments make is not thereby possessing himself of the music. Perhaps no one can do that unless he hears the noises; but there is something else that he must do as well. Our ordinary word for this other thing is listening; and the listening which we have to do when we hear the noises made by musicians is... rather like the thinking we have to do when we hear the noises made, for example, by a person lecturing on a scientific subject.

And pursuing this analogy (which he admits is not exact):

In each case what we get out of it is something which we have to reconstruct in our own minds, and by our own efforts; something which remains for ever inaccessible to a person who cannot or will not make efforts of the right kind, however completely he hears the sounds that fill the room in which he is sitting.

Music, then, and the other arts are systems of ideas, originally brought into existence by the creative imagination of the composer or poet, and distributed, broadcast, to be shared. Such ideas can be grasped by us only through a reproduction of the creative imagination, without which we cannot have within ourselves the idea that the composer or poet had. Our imagination works to recreate the original idea, as far as we are capable of doing so. We may be reminded of how Coleridge believed that we recognize a poet of genius: 'You feel him to be a poet inasmuch as for a time he has made you one, an active creative being' (see p. 43). However, it is not only to works of art, poems, pictures or pieces of music that we attend. We can look at, and listen to, objects in the world, non-artefacts. If Collingwood is right in saying that conscious attention involves not mere sensation, but the double object, ourselves and that which we see or hear (and this is his inheritance from Kant), then it .should follow that what we attend to in the natural world also becomes an idea, not a mere impression. The world is converted, and made part of our system of categories and values by our attention to it.

In so far as 'what we attend to', or 'what we have attended to' is something categorized as a 'thing', something not fleeting but continuous, which we can come back to again and again, whether it is physically in front of our eyes or not, the object of attention must involve not imagination only, but memory, that aspect of imagination specifically assigned to our own continuous past. No animal, human or non-human could recognize an object as continuous, the same object that it had experienced before, without the use of memory. However, to say this is not to embrace a Berkeleian idealism, according to which the whole world is nothing but ideas, whether ideas of memory or of imagination. The word 'idea' is hopelessly inadequate in this context, for it inevitably suggests to us something wholly 'mental' or 'subjective'; and it seems to entail a distinction between an 'idea' and 'that *of* which it is an idea', which is equally misleading. Once again, we are faced with an erosion of the distinction between the 'inner' and the 'outer', the 'given' and our contribution to it. Such a sharp dichotomy, as I hope to have suggested already, did not survive post-Kantian Romanticism, and could not have survived it.

Collingwood, then, is one twentieth-century philosopher who, following the by now traditional post-Kantian path, blurred the line between the inner and the outer. Coming from a different point, but still a part of this tradition, Jean-Paul Sartre reached similar conclusions in his early literary and philosophical works. (I have treated this subject at some length in another place: see my *Imagination*, Faber, 1976, Pt IV. I must return to it here, though from a somewhat different standpoint, since it forms a central step in my present argument.)

In 1938, Sartre took a year away from teaching in order to study recent German philosophy. He was especially interested in the movement known as Phenomenology. This had its origins in the nineteenth century. In 1874 Franz Brentano published a book called *Psychology from an Empirical Point of View*. In this he propounded the theory that the difference between the subject matter of, say, geology or ornithology and that of psychology lay in the fact that consciousness, the subject matter of psychology, unlike rock formations or birds, was always consciousness *of* something. This characteristic of consciousness he referred to by the medieval term Intentionality. Later, Brentano became very much preoccupied by the question of what one was to say about consciousness when it was directed to a fictitious or non-existent object, or indeed an abstract object, such as justice. Was one obliged to say that such objects existed, in order to be, as it were, the targets of consciousness? Did they exist in an altogether different way from that in which rocks and birds exist? But before he reached this perplexing point, Brentano, by the simple enunciation of the principle 'consciousness must be consciousness of something' had reintroduced the external world into the account he gave of perception itself. It was no longer permissible to think of perception in the way that Descartes, Locke, Berkeley and Hume had, as a series of internal ideas about which a question could be raised whether they were related to anything at all. If they were ideas, then, according to Brentano, they were necessarily related to something other than themselves. They had a built-in referent. The difference between this method of validating a reference to an outer world and that of Kant is considerable. Kant, though entitling us to claim knowledge of a world shared between and common to all rational creatures, committed himself only to this being a world of shared appearances. He claimed nothing whatever in the way of knowledge of the real world that might lie behind these appearances. Moreover, his account of perception and of knowledge purported to be wholly *a priori*, explanatory of our experience but not derived from it, but from certain logical necessities. Brentano, in contrast, was interested, as the title of his book proclaimed, in empirical psychology. He was concerned to describe what it was actually like to perceive and to think. And pursuing this line, he found that it is 'precisely through the "appearances" that the appearing thing itself is given to the phenomenologist' (H. Spiegelberg, *The Phenomenological Movement*, Martinus Nijhoff, 1965, p. 147). This is why the introduction of the real world into the world of ideas or impressions seemed like a fresh start, owing nothing to Kant. Whether, in the end, the gulf between them was so wide is a matter of opinion. I find it hard to interpret Kant's *Critique of Pure. Reason* in so purely a non-psychological and non-empirical way as it was doubtless intended. I shall return briefly to this point in chapter 6. But whatever the truth may be, there is no doubt that Phenomenology introduced a fresh atmosphere into European philosophy.

It was not Brentano himself, however, but a follower of his, Edmund Husserl, who was most influential in spreading the phenomenological gospel, in so far as it was spread. His publications spanned the years 1901 to 1931, and his ideas developed considerably during that time. He took his start from Brentano's definition of consciousness. Consciousness was that which was directed onto objects. It was therefore fundamental to his thought that people who perceived (and indeed other animals who perceived) and perceptible physical objects were all in the same world together. That people were conscious of stones or trees certainly served to make them different from the stones or trees themselves. But it did not make them total aliens in the world. They, the perceivers, were physical objects themselves, though of a peculiar kind. Like Brentano, he held that to speak of awareness or consciousness entailed the existence of a world, both an outer and an inner world. Indeed, he became less and less interested in drawing any distinction between the two.

In his later works, Husserl was primarily concerned with what he sometimes called Pure Phenomenology, that is the manner in which, in perceiving or thinking about the world, people ascribe significance to what they perceive or think about. He argued that the content of consciousness, what we immediately see and hear, always points beyond itself to something more general, and therefore more significant and less momentary. In a series of lectures delivered first in 1907, but subsequently much altered, and not published until after his death (Husserl, *Die Idee der Phanomenologie*, Martinus Nijhoff, 1947; see also Husserl, *Leçons phenomenologiques sur la conscience interne du temps* cited in Sartre, *The Psychology of Imagination*, Methuen, 1972, p. 84), he considers the case of someone hearing a sustained musical note. If the hearer tried to isolate and describe the content of his consciousness at a particular moment, he would certainly be aware of hearing a sound at that moment. But he could not accurately describe what he heard except as a part of a sustained note. What he heard at a particular moment, that is, goes beyond the moment, and points to something else, the context that makes sense of it. A sustained note is more than a series of seconds filled with sound. The conscious person, in this case the listener, thus emerges not only as someone who is part of the world and conscious of it, but also as someone who actively constructs this world, and renders it intelligible to himself, and gives it meanings by referring it to the past and the future. For the way in which these meanings are given is largely through the concept of duration; and it is this which is brought to 'bare' perception by the imagination of the perceiver (as Hume dimly recognized). In the notebooks which Husserl kept during the 1930s, there is a great deal about the awareness of time, and the temporal context by providing which the imagination and memory together render the world intelligible. Finally, in the last phase of his philosophical life, he became more and more interested in what we may call the sociology of knowledge. He raised the question of the extent to which the world we interpret for ourselves must also be interpreted so as to be intelligible and significant for more people than one, as part of a socially determined network.

These were some of the ideas that Sartre came across in Germany. He came back to France in a state of high excitement. In 1939 he published a short article in the *Nouvelle Revue Française* in which he proclaimed with powerful rhetoric the revolution in philosophy that he had discovered. (The original article was translated by Joseph P. Fell and printed in the *Journal of the British Society for Phenomenology*, vol. 1, no. 2, May 1970, pp. 4–5). Against what he called 'digestive' philosophy, in which objects perceived are sucked into the mind, to become mental entities, 'ideas' or 'impressions', he found that 'Husserl persistently affirms that one cannot dissolve things in consciousness. You see this tree, to be sure. But you see it just where it is: at the side of the road, in the midst of the dust, alone and writhing in the heat, eight miles from the Mediterranean coast. It could not *enter* your consciousness.' Knowledge, Sartre continued, no longer has to be compared with possession. 'All at once', he wrote, 'consciousness is purified, it is clear as a strong wind. There is nothing in it but a movement of fleeing itself, a sliding beyond itself. If, impossible though it be, you could enter "into" consciousness you would be seized by a whirlwind and thrown back outside, in the thick of the dust near the tree. For consciousness has no inside.' And there was an even greater promised liberation. Our contact with the real world is allowed at last to be more than bare perception. 'For Husserl and the phenomenologists', he wrote,

> our consciousness of things is by no means limited to knowledge of them. Knowledge, or pure 'representation' is only one of the possible forms of my consciousness 'of' this tree; I can also love it, hate it, fear it... so it is that all at once hatred, love, fear – all these famous 'subjective' reactions which were floating in the malodorous brine of the mind are pulled out. They are merely ways of discovering the world. It is things which abruptly reveal themselves to us as hateful, sympathetic, horrible, lovable... Husserl has restored things to their horror and their charm. He has restored to us the world of artists and prophets; frightening, hostile, dangerous, with its havens of mercy and love.

His passionate welcome ended with these words:

> We are ... delivered from the 'internal life'. In vain would we
> seek the carresses and fondlings of our intimate selves...like
> a child who kisses his own shoulder, since everything is finally
> outside, everything even ourselves. Outside, in the world, among
> others. It is not in some hiding-place that we will discover
> ourselves; it is on the road, in the town, in the midst of the
> crowd, a thing among things, a man among men.

Husserl, then, following Brentano, held that consciousness
was to be defined by its being intentional, that is directed upon
an object. There could be no such thing as consciousness that
was not consciousness *of*. But consciousness may be directed
in exactly the same way towards tables and chairs, towards
human passions or sensations, towards ideas or images. Sartre,
taking over this phenomenological doctrine, believed that this
insight unified the world. Humans differ from other things only
by the possession of consciousness, which they can direct upon
objects experienced as distant or near, frightening or reassuring,
hateful or delightful. Humans are, in short, conscious of themselves as occupying a variety of different relations with other
things in the same world. Thus instead of there being a separate
world of 'mental entities', ideas, emotions and so on, such
entities are simply human attributes, in a single world. There
remains no gap to be filled, whether by the imagination or
by any other means, between the inner and the outer worlds.
Consciousness, though in one sense a great divider of humans
from other things, even other animals, is nevertheless one
phenomenon among others in this single world.

When Sartre got back from Germany, he began, while still
inspired by this great vision, to write about imagination. In
The Psychology of Imagination he considers in detail the way
in which we form images of the world, though he insists that
the image must not be thought of as a separable internal object
of attention, but rather a way of thinking of the world itself,
a kind of analogue of the thing thought of. The imagination
is, he argues, our means of thinking of things that are absent,
whether in time or in space; and in so thinking we devise for
ourselves a kind of surrogate object, the visual or auditory or

tactile features of the object itself. This is what we refer to when we speak of the images of imagination. The power of imagination to consider things that are not before our eyes has a further aspect that is central to human life. Humans are, uniquely, free in that they are uniquely capable of thus thinking of things that are not yet, and may never be, before their eyes. This gives them the ability to consider possibilities as well as actualities, the future as well as the present. It also gives them creativity.

Sartre concludes *The Psychology of Imagination* by applying the notion of imaginative consciousness to the understanding of art; and here what he says is extraordinarily close to the views of Collingwood, though it is exceedingly unlikely that he would have read Collingwood's *Principles of Art*. He argues that, just as we see through the performance of a vaudeville actress who is impersonating him on stage to the imaged idea of the absent Maurice Chevalier, so we hear through the performance of a symphony the imagined symphony, which is not present in the concert hall on any particular day, but is something we are, as it were, searching for in the performance, if we attend to it. A bad performance is an obstacle to our hearing the ideal symphony; a good performance, on the other hand, opens our imagination to aspects of the symphony we had missed or failed to grasp before. Sartre concedes that the analogy with the actress and her object, the absent person she is representing on the stage, is not exact. Nevertheless the crucial point is that the aesthetic object, in the case of the symphony, is not the notes on the score, nor the sounds the musicians produce. Just as the painter, in actually laying paint on canvas, has constructed a material analogue of such a kind that everyone, provided he attends to the canvas, can grasp the image the painter had, so the composer, by publishing his work and causing it to be played, has constructed a material analogue for the aesthetic object which is essentially, both for him and the audience, an object of the imagination. Sartre says 'it follows that beauty is a value applicable only to the imaginary'. (*The Psychology of Imagination*, p. 225). (Collingwood's words are 'the music is not the collection of noises, it is the tune in the composer's head. The noises made by the performers and heard by the audience are not the music at all; they are only the means by which the audience, if they listen intelligently, can reconstruct for themselves the imaginary tune' (*Principles of Art*, p. 139).)

I want now to consider a case, described in detail by Sartre, which is less purely aesthetic than watching a theatrical performance, looking at a painting or listening to a symphony. For Sartre believed, as Husserl, and indeed Collingwood did, that we need to bring our interpreting imagination to bear on the visual, auditory or tactual experiences of ordinary life if we are to understand the nature of the world through our own experience. And that we can do this is part of the great phenomenological vision that he carried with him from Germany into his own philosophy.

My next example, then, is taken from Sartre's philosophical novel, *La Nausée* (*Nausea*, trans. L. Alexander, Hamish Hamilton, 1962). The central character of the book, Antoine Roquentin, keeps a diary in which he records his own horrified states of mind, his disgust, despair and sense of futility; and he also records his discoveries about the nature of existence in the world. (Sartre later reported that this character was, absolutely, himself.) He discovers that existence and the words we use to classify it, tidy it up and manage it are quite separate from one another. Such classificatory devices are futile attempts to fend off existence itself, and keep it at bay. This revelation comes to him one day when he sits in a park, looking at the great black roots of a chestnut tree. 'Never until the last few days', he says to himself,

> had I understood the meaning of 'existence' ... when I believed I was thinking about it, I was thinking nothing, my head was empty...Even when I looked at things I was miles from dreaming that they existed... I picked them up in my hands, they served me as tools, I foresaw their hardness. But that all happened on the surface. If anyone had asked me what existence was, I would have answered in good faith that it was nothing, simply an empty form that was added to external things without changing anything in their nature. Then all of a sudden there it was, clear as day; existence had suddenly unveiled itself. It had lost the harmless look of an abstract category. It was the very paste of things. This root was kneaded into existence. Or rather the root, the park gates, the bench on which I sat,

the sparse grass, all that had vanished: the diversity of things, their individuality were only an appearance, a veneer. This veneer had melted, leaving soft monstrous masses, all in disorder, naked in a frightful obscene nakedness. (*Nausea*, pp. 171–3)

Roquentin was seeing through the appearances of things that he labelled 'root', 'bench' or 'grass' to the undifferentiated mass that the world is, behind the veneer of language and man-made convenience-categories. It was the discovery of this reality that appalled him.

At the end of the book there is a ray of light, of sanity and a kind of cheerfulness. Roquentin realizes that, apart from appearances, there is not only the chaotic sucking messiness of 'things-in-themselves' (to whose reality words could not penetrate) but there are also permanent realities of the imagination, which are 'above' existence. Having recorded his scorn of people who, like his bourgeois aunt, claim to find comfort in the arts, Roquentin decides to leave his habitual cafe for ever. He is listening for the last time to the song 'Some of these Days' (which is in fact a kind of leitmotif for the whole novel), when the voice sings 'Some of these days/You'll miss me, honey':

Someone must have scratched the record at that point because it makes an odd noise. And there is something that clutches the heart: the melody is absolutely untouched by this tinny coughing of the needle on the record... It is so far – so far behind. I understand that too: the disc is scratched and is wearing out, perhaps the singer is dead; I'm going to leave, I'm going to catch my train. But behind the existence which falls from one present to another, behind these sounds which decompose from day to day, peel off and slip towards death, the melody stays the same, young and firm, like a pitiless witness. (*Nausea*, p. 230)

And so Roquentin decides to become a writer, to acquire a foothold in the world by creating a purely imaginary entity, a work of art, which will persist for ever, like the melody heard and understood through the scratched record.

This novel is an exploration of the way we can, perhaps in certain moods, or by exercising the imagination in certain peculiarly concentrated ways, see through the immediate perceptual data presented to us to what lies behind the world. We can understand what we see or hear in a new way; and in doing so we may know, as Roquentin knew, that something true and real and permanent has been discovered.

Sartre himself, (who, we must remember, was the Roquentin of the novel) in his purely philosophical writings, makes frequent use of ordinary perceptual objects as thus transparent media through which to see the nature of things as they are. I shall take my next examples, not from his works of fiction, however autobiographical they may be, but from his central existentialist philosophical work, *Being and Nothingness*, published in 1943 (*L' Etre et le Neant*, Paris; trans. Hazel Barnes, Methuen, 1957).

At the beginning of *Being and Nothingness*, Sartre attempted to derive from an examination of human consciousness a general theory of the world. Rather as Descartes claimed to have started from the nature of consciousness and its content to prove that thinking things were completely different from physical, or corporeal, things, and that above both stood the necessary existence of God, so Sartre claimed to have shown, by disclosing the nature of consciousness and what it is consciousness of, that there are two different components of existence, on the one hand beings-in-themselves, inert, unconscious things, and, in contrast, beings-for-themselves, people, whose major differentiating characteristic is that they are conscious, and self-conscious. These two kinds of things make up the whole world. There is only one world, but things in it can be thus divided, one kind from the other. Beings-for-themselves, through their consciousness, necessarily place themselves imaginatively at a distance from the world, though they are part of it. They can contemplate both how things are and how they might be, or might have been. This is the same as to say that they possess imagination, through which they can grasp what is not the case as well as what is the case. And imagination, as we have seen, also gives them freedom. They are not set, like beings-in-themselves, in a rigid system of causal laws. Being to some extent set at a distance from the world of nature, being able to distance themselves from it by their powers of imagination, they are able to envisage a future different from the present, and, within limits, decide to pursue whatever future, among those they can envisage, they choose. No actions and no values are given as inevitable. Everything is up for choice. However, humans, beings-for-themselves, find this freedom a burden. They are not able merely to resign themselves to the inevitability of causal laws, but must constantly take decisions about what should happen next, what they should do, and for what, if any, reason; and this endless capacity to choose is almost intolerable to them. They long, at least in some moods, to sink into the undifferentiated inert mass of being-in-itself. They suffer from a sense of the futility and impermanence of all their own classifications of the world, and the values they ascribe to things within it. Therefore they envy inert, senseless matter.

However, besides envying things-in-themselves, which seem to possess full-blown, fully participating existence, without the ironic, detached precariousness of beings-for-themselves, these conscious beings have another attitude. They fear their non-conscious counterparts. They are terrified that they may be sucked down to share the condition of unconsciousness, to become part of the sticky undifferentiated mess that constitutes the world. The most fearful common nightmare of human beings is that they should lose the freedom and control that they have, and be somehow taken over by unconscious beings, instead of being able to control them, manipulate them, neatly categorize them and keep them in their places. And so there are two basic feelings which human beings must inevitably experience, given their ontological position in the world. One is anguish, when they contemplate their own freedom. The other is nausea, or disgust, in the face of an ultimately unintelligible, uncontrollably spreading and threatening nature. This was the nausea Roquentin experienced when he gazed at the black and convoluted roots of the chestnut tree in the park.

Now against this ontological background, Sartre describes certain natural objects in such a way as to make us believe that they are significant, that they mean or point to the relation in which we inevitably stand to them. We have seen how wholly amorphous and all-embracing the existence of the tree-root became for Roquentin, how he seemed to himself to understand for the first time what existence actually was. In *Being and Nothingness* there are other such cases. We perceive certain

objects as 'viscous', that is as sticky, slimy, muddy, and possessed
of the power to suck us into themselves. They create in us a
sense of nausea or revulsion. We need to fight them off if we
are to retain our humanity, our hard-edged ability to categorize
things and arrange them in the way we want. I will quote one
typically lengthy passage (long, but greatly abbreviated in my
quotation; for the effectiveness of Sartre's rhetoric lies in re-
petition and the accumulation of detail):

> The honey which slides off my spoon onto the honey in the jar
> first sculptures the surface by fastening itself on it in relief, and
> its fusion with the whole is presented as a gradual sinking...
> In the substance which dissolves into itself there is a visible
> resistance, like the refusal of an individual who does not want
> to be annihilated...and at the same time a softness pushed to
> its ultimate limit. Throw a viscous substance. Instead of running
> [like water] it draws itself out, it displays itself, it flattens itself
> out, it is SOFT; touch the viscous, and it does not resist, it
> yields. The viscous is compressible. It gives us at first the im-
> pression that it is a being which can be possessed...I can take it
> in my hands...separate a certain quantity of honey...from the
> rest in the jar, and thereby create an individual object...but
> at the same time the softness of this substance which is squashed
> in my hands gives me the impression that I am destroying it.
> The viscous is docile. Only at the very moment when I believe
> that I possess it, behold, by a curious reversal, it possesses me.
> Here appears its essential character; its softness is leech-like...
> Viscosity is the revenge of the in-itself; a sickly-sweet feminine
> revenge which may be symbolized at another level by the quality
> 'sugary'...a sugary viscosity is the ideal of the viscous; it sym-
> bolizes the sugary death of the for-itself, like that of a wasp
> which sinks into the honey and drowns in it. (*Being and Nothing-
> ness*, pp. 608–9)

In embarking on this highly emotive description, and others
of the same kind, Sartre was much influenced by a French
historian of science, Gaston Bachelard, whose book, *The Psycho-
analysis of Fire* had appeared in Paris in 1938 (*La psychanalyse
du feu*, Gallimard, 1938), and who had also written on the significance of water, especially as it occurs in dreams. Bachelard's
general thesis was that the task of science is gradually to sepa-

rate itself from the common idea of material things; and that these common ideas are not based solely on observation but are imbued with emotion. It is not simply that our everyday observations of nature are crude or inaccurate, what might generally be dubbed unscientific, but capable of being made more accurate; they are fundamentally flawed because they are not dispassionate. At a common-sense level we think of material substances as significant to us, and thus our ideas of them, at a pre-scientific level, are connected with the feelings of each individual. Science aims to wean its practitioners from all such emotional commitments. Bachelard referred to such pre-scientific ways of looking at the world as 'the material imagination'.

In *Being and Nothingness*, Sartre rejected this name; but he admitted that this was merely a matter of nomenclature. He accepted Bachelard's thesis whole-heartedly. It fitted entirely with his notion of imagination, as that which enables us to see the significance of things. Like Bachelard, he claimed that there were some things, the viscous, fire, water, which, unless we became scientists, we inevitably saw in a particular emotion-laden way, things which simply *were* the bearers of meaning for us. He was anxious to avoid the charge of merely ascribing to material objects an emotional significance they did not, or did not necessarily, possess (the pathetic fallacy). It was for this reason that he would not use Bachelard's phrase 'the material imagination'. For he feared that the use of 'imagination' in this context, because of its old association with the unreal and the fanciful, might suggest too strongly that what we ascribed, for example, to the honey in the jar was not a real quality of the honey, but an image in our minds. It was essential for his vision of the world that real objects could be perceived by us as actually hateful, loveable, disgusting or attractive. This was what he had learned from Husserl. The disgustingness must not come from within. Yet he writes (*Being and Nothingness*, p. 603) of the real qualities of objects being 'symbols' of their nature; and, for the interpretation of symbols, he would admit that we need imagination if we are to see through them to what they signify. Thus it seems he ought to have admitted that the imagination has a part to play when we perceive an object as, let us say, disgusting. At any rate, there need be no general prohibition against saying that when Sartre tells us how the viscous reveals to us the nature of the world, he is talking not merely of perception, but of perception imbued with imagination.

I have suggested that Sartre's peculiar rhetoric, his philosophical style, depends on the building up of detailed descriptions so that we can see and feel the characteristics he wants to impress on us as ontologically important. There is another way in which Sartre actually uses imaginative inventions to make us accept philosophical points. This is the method of using a story or anecdote in place of an argument. Philosophers frequently make use of examples in order to make their arguments intelligible; and, especially in moral philosophy, these examples may take the form of an anecdote. But as far as I know Sartre was the only philosopher who seemed to hold that the anecdote was enough, or rather that it was better than an argument. He seemed to be saying 'if you enter into the story, and grasp its meaning, then you will have grasped the truth'. This is more usually the technique of novelists, film-makers or the writers of opera than of philosophers. But it has a bearing on the philosophical question we are concerned with, namely the relation between imagination and truth, and especially timeless truth, expressed in narrative. I will consider, in this connection, Sartre's presentation of the case against solipsism, the sceptical position into which Descartes' so-called Method of Doubt temporarily brought him. The method led to the conclusion that, for all I can know, there might be no one in the universe except myself. For I have nothing but my own perceptions to suggest the existence of other people, and my perceptions are internal to me, with no relation to an outside world that can be proved (see *Meditation* I, *Philosophical Works*, vol. 1, pp. 144–9). It was precisely from the bonds of this kind of scepticism, or even of its possibility, that Sartre claimed that Husserl had for ever freed us. Sartre believed that the solipsistic position was nonsensical. But he argues that as long as we think of the proof of the existence of others as a matter merely of knowledge, then the solipsist's position is impregnable. We can never show that we are in possession of more than an appearance of other people. Instead we must reject pure epistemology, and consider what it is actually like to be human, and indeed to be one human being, myself. After all, Husserl has taught us that we do not merely know things in the world, we react to them.

We must therefore consider the character of my existence in the world and see whether, given that character, it is imaginable that there should be no other humans than myself. And so he embarks on a description of how other people individually impinge on my consciousness and make it what it is. If the description is vivid and persuasive enough, then we may conclude that it is a description of something generally true, we may argue from the particular to the universal. We shall thus reach understanding of the way things are.

There are two parts to Sartre's 'refutation' of solipsism. First, he invites us to consider what it is like to see another human being sitting in a park reading a book. I see this person not merely as a physical object in a certain spatial relation with other physical objects. I see him immediately, without inference, as an object which has a centre of vision of its own. I see him with a stretch of lawn in front of him and recognize immediately that this is a lawn for him as well as for me. 'We are dealing', Sartre writes, 'with a relation without parts, given all in one, within which there unfolds a spatiality that is not my spatiality' (*Being and Nothingness*, p. 254). The man is reading. Now we could try to regard 'reading' as the name of a property the man has for the time being, as a stone may, for the time being, be cold. Yet I understand as I watch him that there is a sense in which the man reading escapes me, as a stone does not. 'At the heart of his visible form, he makes his escape from me'. I cannot see with his eyes, and what he reads cannot strike me in the way it strikes him. He is free of me. So to see a man reading is to see a particular kind of object, which cannot be assimilated to all the other objects I perceive. It is inevitable that I interpret what I see as a 'human person', that is free and beyond my control, living his own life. (We may be reminded here of Strawson's basic particulars, persons, to whom both 'M' and 'P' predicates may be ascribed; see p. 17.)

The second part of the 'refutation' consists of another story (ibid., p. 259). Moved by overwhelming curiosity or jealousy, I am quite unself-consciously looking into a room through the keyhole. I am fully aware of the keyhole, and of my interest in what is going on the other side of the door, but I am not thinking of myself as a separate object. I do not think of myself as an eavesdropper, I just eavesdrop.

But all of a sudden I hear footsteps in the hall. Someone is looking at me. What does this entail? I suddenly become, for myself, exactly and only what I appear to the other person to be...an eavesdropper. I do not reject how-I-appear to the other as a strange or alien image which has nothing to do with me. On the contrary, I recognize the image he has of me, and I accept it with shame.

It is shame, Sartre says,

which reveals to me the other's look and myself at the end of that look. It is shame that makes me live, not know, the situation of being looked at. Now shame is shame of myself. It is the recognition of the fact that I am indeed the object which the other is looking at and judging. I can be ashamed only as my freedom escapes me and I become a given object. Beyond any mere knowledge that I can have, I am the object at which the other person looks.

Moreover, in grasping myself in this new light, as ashamed before someone else, I see myself in a world which has essentially changed to accommodate the other person as well as myself. He sees not only me, but all the other things as well, the door, the keyhole, the walls. All the things which were simply instruments or obstacles for my purposes before, are taken in by him, in a different way, as part of the context in which he places me. 'They turn to him an aspect which I cannot comprehend.'

Sartre draws enormous consequences from the fact that I exist not only for myself, but as an object for other people. The possibility of bad faith, the inevitability of conflict, as each struggles to diminish the other's freedom, both flow from this source. My interest, however, is not in these consequences; it is methodological. In introducing the story of what happens to the eavesdropper, Sartre is inviting us to interpret something, and to see more in it than a simple recognizable story. We are to see that such things could not happen if solipsism were true; and that this truth can be reached by attending not to what we know and can prove, but to what we feel and do not need to prove. Our so-called innermost feelings are our contact with the world. The distinction between inner and outer has become a matter of no importance. The shock of discovering myself under observation is the shock of realizing that I am not and could not be alone in the world, because I am inevitably an object in the world for others. Their existence is as indisputable as my own.

The story, any story, is, as Sartre had argued in *The Psychology of Imagination*, an imaginary construction. In telling this story he invites us to share the image he has made. If we do share it, we will see what it means; for, like all stories, it has a particular point. The author of the story and those who read or hear it see through it to its meaning, and in grasping that meaning, we could say that they have understood the way things are.

Obviously whether the story itself was true, whether such events ever actually happened, is a matter of no importance whatever. Sartre is simply using a literary device to bring us, as he supposes, to a position where we can grasp the truth, that is, that we have to start our thoughts about the world from the acknowledgement that it is a public world, with more people in it than one. The other lesson we have to learn is that we cannot tell one story about what we see and touch, and quite another about how we feel, how we respond to the situation we are in. Our emotional attitudes and our sensations form one whole. The world cannot be perceived without its being given some significance; and it is the function of the imagination to create the meanings that are in the world. This is what Sartre had learned from Husserl. The 'malodorous brine' of the mind had been opened up: loving, hating, fearing and indeed feeling ashamed are all ways of discovering the world.

So can we say, as Sartre wanted us to, that we can read the world as a set of intelligible signs, and thus read not only things that are intended to be signs, such as portraits or impersonations, but objects in the natural world as well? Explaining his programme, he says (*Being and Nothingness*, p. 600) 'We will not look for images, but rather will seek to explain the meaning which really belongs to things'; and again 'material meanings, the human sense of needles, snow, grained wood, of crowded, of greasy, etc. are as real as the world, neither more nor less, and to come into the world is to rise up in the midst of these meanings.' It is true that we are all born into a world full of such meanings. They are our cultural environment. We are taught to eschew the sticky and prefer the clean, to distinguish flowers from weeds, to like the former (more or less), and, mostly, dislike the latter. But there is a remaining sense of possible arbitrariness in ascribing such attitudes to ourselves. How are we to tell whether our way of seeing things is or is not a revelation of an unchangeable truth? How are we to distinguish a *sense* of understanding, a mood, from a real understanding, upon which we may base a truth-claim? Which of our attitudes do we carry with us in our genes, which derive from our upbringing, which, if any, could justify us, Sartre-like, in claiming a revelation of 'human reality' or an insight into ontology? I shall hope to approach rather nearer to an answer to these doubts in the following chapters.

4

The Symbolic

We are searching for a way in which an imaginative interpretation of the world, though in some sense personal and temporal (that is, made by each individual from a particular point of view and at a particular time), may nevertheless be a clue to truths which have wider application. A Cartesian philosophy, according to which each individual is locked in among his own ideas, offered no hope for such generality. Sartre, as we have seen, welcomed Husserl as the saviour of philosophy, believing that he had taken the first great step on the way to such an interpretation, by rescuing philosophy from the futilities and ultimate frustrations of Cartesian dualism. An even more enthusiastic and thorough attempt to deny Cartesianism was made by Sartre's near contemporary, and one-time friend, Maurice Merleau-Ponty. He set out to demonstrate the unity of the inner with the outer world, the one and only world being physical, but entirely and necessarily constructed out of interpretations, emotions and meanings (Merleau-Ponty, *The Phenomenology of Perception*, 1945; English trans. Colin Smith, Routledge & Kegan Paul, 1962). These meanings constitute the only world there is, of which we ourselves are both members and makers. There is no pre-existing 'given' on which we impose or overlay these constructions. Such a theory, according to which we are held to make up the world as we go along, with no *a priori* constraints, might either seem to impose the constructions of one individual on the rest without legitimacy, or to lay the foundation for a total relativism, with no one construction or interpretation being preferred to or privileged above any other. In practice, Merleau-Ponty, like Sartre or indeed Hume, tends on the whole to assume without argument that 'we' construct the world in much the same way as one another, though we might construct it differently. He certainly makes no attempt to prove, as Kant did, that the categories we employ to describe and understand the world are logically necessary.

In the preface to the *Phenomenology of Perception* Merleau-Ponty tells us that phenomenology is the study of essences; but it is also 'a philosophy which puts essences back into existence, and does not expect to arrive at an understanding of man and the world from any starting point other than that of their "facticity" [that is, their existence in time and space]. It is a philosophy for which the world is always "already there", as an inalienable presence' (p. vii). Phenomenology is an attempt to describe, as exactly as possible, what it is like to be thus in the world, a part of it, without having recourse to any scientific presuppositions, or any of the assumptions (such as the Cartesian assumption that the 'I' who thinks is the essential starting point for analysis) which are usually made by philosophers. Philosophers who start with 'states of consciousness' and who then have to try to find criteria by which to distinguish the 'real' from the 'imaginary' are, he says, simply overlooking the phenomena of the world.

> If I am able to talk about 'dreams' and 'reality', to bother my head about the distinction between imaginary and real...it is because this distinction is already made by me before any analysis; it is because I have an experience of the real as of the imaginary, and the problem then becomes one...of making explicit our primordial knowledge of the 'real', of describing our perception of the world as that upon which our idea of truth is forever based. (p. xvi)

Following this programme, then, Merleau-Ponty first has to reject the account of perception to be found in Descartes, that all perceptions are 'in' the mind, as part of that mind's furniture of ideas (the other part of the furniture being innate). Then he must reject Hume's theory of perception according to which what we receive from the world is supposed to be a series of internal impressions which have somehow to be 'objectified', through the mysterious but universal workings of the imagination. What is wrong with this theory is the fundamental assumption that we could in any circumstances be aware of a 'pure' impression. It seems harmless enough to introduce the word 'impression' to cover sensations and perceptual experiences such as that of redness. But in fact it is an error from which the whole fatal divorce between the outer and the inner worlds derives. 'It is unnecessary to show', Merleau-Ponty says, 'since most authors are agreed on it, that the notion [of a pure impression] corresponds to nothing in our experience...but this does not dispose of the question why we feel justified in theory in distinguishing within experience a layer of "impressions"' (*Phenomenology of Perception*, p. 4). He argues that in fact we are not so justified. For the very concept of perception involves picking out something against a background. What we perceive, however simplified, always forms part of a 'field'. And so the notion of an instantaneous 'pure' impression is contradictory. If there were such a thing it would be imperceptible. The idea of picking something out within a 'field' introduces a further element in perception, that of the significance to us of what we claim to perceive. According to Merleau-Ponty, the apprehension of this significance is an integral part of perception. We have no need to ascribe it to any particular intellectual faculty. There is no need to invoke, as Hume did, the concept of imagination to fulfil this function.

In the critique of earlier theories of perception, Kant fares no better than Descartes or Hume. It is because Kant still held that, to explain our knowledge of the world, we need to start from the 'I' who perceives, and discover the role of the various faculties of the mind by the use of which the separate, observing 'I' organizes and gains knowledge of the world that Merleau-Ponty, and Phenomenology, has to reject Kant's philosophy, as well as Hume's. Kant's central figure, as we have seen, is in some ways the progenitor of the Romantic hero. He is still separate from the world he perceives, in some ways alienated from it. Merleau-Ponty writes:

It is true that, in Kant, empirical psychologism has been left behind, that the meaning and structure of the percept are no longer the mere outcome of psycho-physiological events, that rationality is no longer a fortunate accident bringing together dispersed sensations. But although [what we perceive] may be

expressible in terms of some law, this law must not be considered as a model on which the phenomena are built up...
It is not because their form produces a state of...maximum
coherence and, in the Kantian sense, makes a world possible that
these objects enjoy a privileged place in our perception. Perceptions are the very coming into being of the world and not
the condition of its possibility; it is the birth of the law, not
something realized according to the law; it is the identity of the
external and the internal and not the projection of the internal
on the external. (ibid., p. 61)

Such a unification of the world, then, stems from the anti-
Cartesian refusal to split human beings, those who perceive the
world, into two parts, the mind and the body. All the qualities
we ascribe to objects spring into existence as we perceive them.
We do not sense them and then externalize them. In his last
published work, *The Eye and the Mind* (reprinted in *Aesthetics*,
ed. Harold Osborne, OUP, 1972, p. 55), Merleau-Ponty echoes
the words of Sartre:

Visible and mobile, my body is a thing among things; it is caught
in the fabric of the world, and its cohesion is that of a thing.
But because it moves itself and sees, it holds things in a circle
round itself. Things are an annexe or prolongation of itself; they
are incrusted into its flesh, they are parts of its full definition;
the world is made of the same stuff as the body.

This is the full-blown rhetoric of the One World. My perception
of the world needs no medium through which I can translate
what I receive through my senses into conceptual or emotional
understanding; nor is there any need of a mechanism to assure
me that what I see and hear relates to an external world. Hume
agreed with Merleau-Ponty that the existence of the world is
something we take for granted in all our reasonings; but he still
thought it proper to ask what causes induce us to believe in
this world so implicitly. Merleau-Ponty simply asserted that such
an enquiry was meaningless. The world is not what I think but
what I live through; and what we perceive is what things are.

Yet despite the exhilaration of this new realism, the fact
remains that each individual has his own outlook on the world.

And it may often seem that these outlooks are extremely diverse. It cannot be denied that we may perceive different aspects of things, and that their significance may strike us as a meaning which can be apprehended differently according, for example, to how much we know of them, or with what other things we connect them. As Kant argued, the empirical, as opposed to the *a priori*, imagination depends for its deliverances upon the experiences we happen to have had. Merleau-Ponty says 'The significance of a thing inhabits that thing as the soul inhabits the body: it is not behind the appearance' (*Phenomenology of Perception* p. 31). We may agree with this in so far as we would agree that often, if something appears significant to us, we could not detach the significance from the appearance; the thing has a 'meaning', as it has other properties. But Merleau-Ponty is shifting about here between different senses of 'having a meaning'. He gives an example (ibid., p. 17) in which I am walking along the seashore towards a ship that has run aground, and at first the masts of the ship merge into the forest which borders the sand dunes. But there will be a moment when these details suddenly become part of the ship, and I cannot understand how I ever saw them otherwise. Here the 'meaning' of what I see is 'the top part of a ship', and the meaning dawns on me as I get closer. On the other hand, elsewhere he uses the concept of 'meaning' in the way that Sartre does when he speaks of 'material meanings', 'the human sense of snow, grained wood, of crowded, greasy, etc.' (see p. 63). Criticizing the empiricists for supposing that, when we speak of a landscape as sad or dismal we are projecting our own inner feelings onto what we see, Merleau-Ponty suggests that we shall understand the nature of perception only if we recognize that the landscape is gloomy in exactly the same way as it is grey or flat. He deliberately refuses, that is to say, the distinction drawn by Hume, between the steady and universal principles of imagination and those which may be merely childish and poetical. Hume, as we have seen, did not succeed in making clear what was the basis of this distinction; and I am not proposing that, in thinking about our interpretation of perception, we should insist on a hard line between the inevitable and ordinary on the one side and the fanciful or creative on the other. Nevertheless, it is essential to allow that, while some interpretations of what we see, hear or touch seem necessary and common to everyone, there are others in making which we enter into a more creative relation with our senses, where we seek to draw a significance from what they give us which is in some way hidden, and which we feel would be illuminating, if it could only be extracted. Thus, though we might agree that the judgement that a landscape is gloomy is based on the features it has, such as flatness, the fact remains that while everyone would agree that it was flat, they might not agree on the 'meaning' of this flatness.

In this sense, the meanings things have are not always universal, that is, common to everyone. There seems to be a kind of sliding scale of degrees of interpretation, from the genuinely common and inevitable to the downright eccentric. And we may ask both why we interpret something in one way rather than another, and, more important, whether one person may not interpret it quite differently from another.

Pursuing this point will, I hope, throw some light on our goal, which is to link a common and essentially timeless understanding with imagination. For though both Merleau-Ponty and Sartre wish to exclude imagination from perception, on the grounds that it would reintroduce a whiff of faculty psychology, as well as the Cartesian concentration on the inner life, which they believe they have triumphantly thrown out, yet it seems to me impossibly difficult to describe what we mean by 'interpretation' or the 'grasping of significance' if we are debarred from using the concept of imagination; nor can there be any harm in using it, as long as we recognize that we are not speaking of a separate faculty, but rather a way in which perception and thought are intermingled, accompanied, as often as not, by emotion. It has indeed become something of a philosophical truism (though none the less true for that) that, in perception, thought in varying degrees intermingles with sight and hearing and also with the framing of images or ideas of the absent or invented; and that it is along this spectrum of mental activity that we must place imagination. Partially following both Hume and Kant, we may use the term 'imagination' for any of the activities along the spectrum.

The source of many recent discussions of imagination, whether in epistemological or aesthetic contexts, and from which the truism I have just stated largely derives, is a section of Wittgenstein's *Philosophical Investigations* where he discusses 'seeing an aspect' and 'seeing as' (Ludwig Wittgenstein, *Philosophical Investigations*, trans. G. E. M. Anscombe, Oxford, 1953, pp. 193–214). Wittgenstein starts the passage with this example (p. 193): 'I contemplate a face, and then suddenly notice its likeness to another. I see that it has not changed; and yet I see it differently. I call this experience "noticing an aspect". Its causes are of interest to psychologists. We are interested in the concept and its place among other concepts of experience.' He goes on to consider the case of an ambiguous or puzzle picture, which one may see either as a duck or as a rabbit. When we switch from seeing it as one to seeing it as the other we are connecting it, he says, in different ways to other images (of ducks or of rabbits). And when we report how we see it, we are expressing a change of aspect we have noticed. Wittgenstein says 'the expression of a change of aspect is the expression of a new perception, and at the same time of the perception's not being changed'. Later (p. 212) he says 'what I perceive in the dawning of an aspect is not a property of the object, but an internal relation between it and other objects. It is almost as if "seeing the sign in this context" were the echo of a thought, "the echo of a thought in sight" one would like to say.' And again (p. 213): 'The concept of an aspect is akin to the concept of an image. In other words: the concept "I am now seeing it as..." is akin to "I am now having this image". Doesn't it take imagination to hear something as a variation on a particular theme? And yet one is perceiving something in so hearing it.'

I would, then, following Wittgenstein, contend that we need the idea of imagination as a bridge between what we see or hear and what we may claim to be a true interpretation of that seeing or hearing. Although, as is usual with Wittgenstein, what he writes is suggestive rather than conclusive, and not all that he says is internally consistent, yet I believe that there is an idea here which is central to any attempt we may make to describe our understanding of the world. This is the idea of perception imbued with thought, perception that is interpreted, at one end of the continuum, in quite routine ways, or, further along the same continuum, in one of two possible ways, (as in the duck-rabbit case) or, further along still, in more bizarre or inventive ways.

It may be argued that in the case of a trick drawing where there are just two ways the drawing can be seen, and where it is specifically ambiguous as to whether the drawing represents a duck or a rabbit, when we see it as one or the other we can be agreed to be interpreting it rightly, in one of the two permitted ways. In contrast, there must be many cases of seeing something as something else where there is no correctness or rightness about it. My imagination may lead me astray. I may see something as what it simply is not. For example, I may see a shadow as the lurking figure of a burglar, or hear the cry of a gull as a voice calling my name. Such an argument would lead to the conclusion that we are still just as far as ever from a way in which we can present our interpretations of perception as justifying a truth-claim. Wittgenstein gives the example of a child who, as part of a game, says that a chest is a house. In treating the chest as a house (and, as Wittgenstein says 'thereafter it is interpreted as a house in every detail') is the child seeing the chest as a house? Here is a case, it seems to me, when we might say that imagination takes over from perception. In so far as the chest is being used as a surrogate house, its perceptual qualities cease to be of any interest, except as they place some restrictions on the kind of house that is imagined (if, for example, the house is a doll's house, the chest may represent a mansion with many rooms; if it is an ordinary house for humans, not dolls, then inevitably it will feature as a small house).

Other instances in which the perceived qualities of the object that is actually seen become irrelevant, because of the strength of the imaginative interpretation, may be drawn from psychiatrists' descriptions of delusions. There are, for example, some kinds of delusion which are based on perception, but in the grip of which the patient's judgement of what that perception means is, we should say, completely irrational, or obviously false. In his book *General Psychopathology* (trans. Huenig and Hamilton, Manchester University Press, 1963, pp. 55–137) Karl Jaspers, a philosopher turned psychiatrist, gives a number of exact descriptions of hallucinations (false perceptions) and delusions (persistent false beliefs). Jaspers argues that our concept of reality depends for its existence on our perceptions of the world as separate from ourselves, and as the context within which we live and act. 'But', he adds, 'the reality itself which we meet in practice is always an interpretation, a meaning; the meaning of things, events or situations' (p. 94). In an abnormal psychological state 'suddenly things seem to mean something quite different. The patient sees two people in the street in raincoats: they ARE Schiller and Goethe. There are scaffoldings up on some houses: the whole town is going to be demolished. Another patient sees a man in the street; she knows at once that he is an old lover of hers; he looks quite different, it is true; he has disguised himself with a wig. But still it is he, though he looks a bit odd.' Such interpretations, based on perfectly ordinary perception (the Schiller and Goethe pair, for example, would be described by the patient in the same language that anyone would use to describe two men in macintoshes) are wild interpretations of perception. Similar delusions may give rise to the idea that everyone is talking about the patient or laughing at him; and these beliefs may be based on words actually overheard in the street, but wrongly interpreted as to their reference. We know quite well that the chest the children are playing in and treating as a house is not a house. So in a way do they, and when they are bored with their game they will not think of the chest except in the way they have seen it all along (at least in one common meaning of 'see'). The difference between them and the psychiatric patients whom Jaspers describes is their degree of insight into how they are interpreting what they see, and whether they are consciously and deliberately indulging in play.

And so we must persist in asking by what criteria we can validate an interpretation of a perceptual experience. Very often the interpretation will be obvious; and we would find no difficulty in getting other people to corroborate it. This would be the case in Merleau-Ponty's example, where we walk towards a grounded boat and begin to see it 'as' a boat, not a part of the forest. But if we venture into a more idiosyncratic interpretation of what we see or hear, how can we justify the feeling we may have that we have reached understanding by means of it, that our interpretation amounts to the truth? The paranoid patient, after all, claims that his interpretation of what he sees and hears all 'fits in': all goes to show that he is subject to suspicion and persecution; and he holds this belief with unshakeable conviction. But we say it is a delusion.

And here we come to an important distinction. If the child at play persisted in an actual belief that the chest was a house, rather than that he was merely using it as a house or pretending it was a house, then we should have to say that the child was deluded. Of course, the concept of pretending is not simple; and there are doubtless cases which might hover between pretending, or acting, and being deluded. We should certainly expect to find such wobbly distinctions not only among children, who may forget what is 'pretend' and what real, but also among psychiatric patients who may sometimes only half believe their own false ideas or wrong interpretations, or at any rate hold them at the same time as holding other rational but incompatible beliefs. Nevertheless, on the whole we can distinguish what is a valid and what an invalid, fanciful or plain false interpretation of experience. Just as we recognize a dog as a dog by fitting its appearance and behaviour into that of other dogs (and Hume thought our imagination went round the world on our behalf fetching together images of other dogs for us to use for comparison) so, for the most part, our interpretations of perceptions are subject to testing against what would generally be held to be probable or possible. We know that the two men in raincoats cannot be Goethe and Schiller, who are long dead. We think it quite probable that we shall never know who they are, or that they are two men from the gas company. If someone says 'They are Goethe and Schiller all the same' there is no further means of persuasion available. We have to think either that, intelligibly, the speaker is playing a game – she has just given the two men these names because they are always seen together or because they look like Romantic writers, or else that she is just saying that they are Goethe and Schiller without really believing it. But if the rest of her behaviour seems to show that she does believe it, then we say she is suffering from a delusion. It is difficult, if not impossible, for us to share a genuinely baseless or bizarre belief. Suppose someone looks out at my lawn and says 'How lovely: you've got mushrooms growing there. Let's have some for supper.' I look out and see what she sees. But I say 'Alas: they are not mushrooms. They are inedible toadstools.' And we go out and I show her that if we look at their undersides, they are not the right colour for mushrooms. In this case I can understand her interpretation of what she saw, and how it led her not only to a false identification but to a whole series of lovely images of wild mushrooms cooking and the smell there would be in the kitchen and how well they would go with our bacon. All these images go to make up the meaning she gave to what she saw on my lawn. But both she and I have an agreed way to demonstrate that her interpretation was mistaken, and the meaning she understood did not really belong to what she saw. She can say 'I see now that I was wrong, but from the window I took them to be mushrooms.'

Now the case of mistaking toadstools for mushrooms is a particularly clear case; and I am far from suggesting that the way you interpret your perceptual experiences must always be the way I would. The Duke of Wellington, at Salamanca, observing an injudicious movement of the enemy said, 'Now we have them'. (See P. F. Strawson's *'Imagination and Perception'* in *Freedom and Resentment*, Methuen, 1974, p. 57.) I, being ignorant of strategy, could not have said what Wellington said, on the basis of a perceived movement of the enemy troops. Nevertheless, he could have made me see it, if he had had time. He could have explained how he could see defeat for the enemy in what looked to me like just a bit of shuffling about.

This will turn out to be a matter of great importance in the consideration of what truth we may claim to have reached from our imaginative interpretations, or those of others. The truth is what we claim to have reached when we 'see' or 'grasp' how things are, and how they hang together. The paranoid 'understands' how all the words she hears and the expressions she sees on people's faces hang together under the hypothesis that she is the centre of a plot, that she is being victimized. She would claim to know this, as the truth. Other people cannot share that reading of the situation. It does not fit in with the rest of what we know or assume about the way the world is. (Of course, sometimes we assume that someone is subject to paranoid delusions when they really are being persecuted. This is a familiar plot in novels. The expected is not always what happens; and we might sometimes have to blame ourselves not only for undue scepticism, but for lack of imagination, if we consistently poohpoohed what turned out to be a genuine reason for alarm.) When a new and bold interpretation is given of a perceptual phenomenon, then people may be brought to accept it because, either at once or after due explanation, it may seem to illuminate other things that are accepted, or to explain them. John Casey, in his book *The Language of Criticism* (Methuen, 1966, pp. 17–19) discusses this kind of acceptance in an attempt to throw light on acceptance in the sphere of aesthetics or criticism. However, he starts by taking an analogous example from science (or perhaps the mythology of science). He says:

> Newton, in seeing the apple fall saw the possibility of explaining 'the fall of apples and the like'. And so the movement of the planets was connected with the fall of apples. No new facts had been discovered but the concept of 'falling' had been enriched by being applied for the first time to the whole solar system. The motions of the heavenly bodies had been 'explained' by their being connected with those of earthly ones, and a new application had been found for the concept of 'falling'. At the same time an 'explanation' had been provided of what it is for earthly objects to fall, by connecting their movements with the movements of the planets.

This, whether a true story or not, is an instance of what Coleridge would call the 'shaping' power of imagination, that is the power of seeing through an ordinary perceptual phenomenon to something of which now it becomes only an illustration. And this explanation, this system which has been revealed, is not a delusion, because it actually succeeds in bringing together in one explanatory framework things that had hitherto been separate. Moreover, as an explanation, Newton's also had the great advantage that it worked. It turned out to be a useful tool in all kinds of other predictions and calculations.

Casey argues that such reasoning, if we may so think of it, as lay behind Newton's perception was not inductive or deductive reasoning, and was not capable of proof. Our acceptance of it is what he calls 'aesthetic'. We somehow see, or accept, that it is right. We understand. Some explanations are in this way acceptable, others are not. He writes:

> If you prove that the ponds on a certain piece of land drain into a lake some miles away by pouring a coloured liquid into

the pond and finding it later in the lake, your decision to believe that the liquid travelled underground rather than that a
meteorite carrying an identical liquid fell into the lake is equally
'aesthetic'. The frame of explanation carried by the latter account
would be too clumsy ramshackle and 'unnatural'. The account
itself would be far-fetched and improbable, just as a dream
interpretation by Freud, or a Shakespearian interpretation by
Wilson Knight or for that matter a metaphor of Crashaw's might
be far-fetched or improbable. (ibid., p. 21)

Now it seems to me that to say of an explanation that it
is 'far-fetched' is a real objection to accepting it, whether as
an explanation of a natural phenomenon, or of the meaning of
a text, or of a metaphor. And we must notice that the intelligibility of such an objection presupposes that there is, as it were,
a shared world of the probable, the likely, the homely or the
familiar, of things that have genuine and observable similarities
with one another, beyond which the proposed 'explanation'
strays. We assume a shared sense of what is possible, and what
are real connections between things; for example, of what
may be comprehended under the expression 'and the like' if, as
Newton was, we are concerned to make an observation of
'apples and the like'. Such shared presumptions can be referred
to as 'common sense'. It may be better to think of them as a
common culture. Their existence is of the greatest importance in
what follows.

Yet we have already seen that the creative imagination, the
imagination of genius, is not wholly bound by the constraints
of this common culture of probabilities. The question is how
far can it stray, in seeking understanding? In a previous chapter
(see p. 30) I quoted Kant as saying that the imagination is
'a powerful agent for creating as it were a second nature out
of the material supplied to it by the first nature'. The creative
imagination is free from the constraints imposed by the laws of
understanding on our perceptions of nature itself; and therefore
out of this borrowed material it can create something else,
'namely what surpasses nature'. Kant calls these representations
of the creative imagination 'ideas' because they cannot be apprehended in the appearances of things in the way that objects
that conform to natural laws can be. Kant uses the expression

'idea' in a special or technical sense for something which cannot be experienced directly, but can serve as a kind of ideal, lying outside the reign of the laws of nature (or of reason) within which experience is necessarily constrained. Thus, the great 'ideas of reason' are ideas of God, Freedom and Immortality, of which we can have no experience. So, the analogous aesthetic ideas of the creative imagination can be sought after, or approached, only as one approaches an ideal. He says 'they strain after something lying out beyond the confines of experience.' The imagination 'finds an expression for what is indefinable, and makes it universally communicable'. Kant refers to this as a unifying process. And that in which, or by the use of which, the expression is found, behind which the indefinable lies, is called a symbol (*Critique of Judgement*, p. 223).

The concept of the symbol as that through which imagination may work is full of ambiguities. I shall try to use the word in a sense that is as near to ordinary use as possible. But in ordinary language itself the word is not unequivocal. For example, algebraic symbols are letters used to stand for unknown or not yet determined numbers. Numerical symbols on the other hand, form part of a wide and varied mathematical notation which we have to learn, just as the elements of musical notation must be learned. These too might be referred to as symbols, but are not regularly so designated any more than are the letters of the alphabet, as they are used, not in algebra, but in ordinary writing. Some have made a case for suggesting that letters are symbols of sounds, and that words are symbols of those things or ideas that they signify. But this is not the way the word 'symbol' is generally understood, nor is it the way I shall use it. What is common to words and symbols, in the normal sense, is that both stand for, or mean, something other than themselves. But we become so accustomed to words that we do not, and need not, on the whole, notice them. We see straight through them to what we understand them to mean, just as, once we have learned to read, we no longer consider the letters out of which we spell the words, but go straight through to the words themselves, and thence to their meaning. In so far as words are like tools, they become tools that are an extension of ourselves, as a violinist's bow seems an extension of his arm.

In any case, language as a whole is better thought of as, in origin at least, more directly expressive than symbolic of something other than itself. Even if each word may have a 'meaning' (and even this is dubious, if we think of words like 'if' and 'but', which cannot be thought to mean anything by themselves: they have functions, rather than referends) we nevertheless first learn to use language as a more sophisticated means of expressing our feelings, or as a more successful method of exercising our will than were the sounds we could make as babies. (For a more detailed discussion of this point, see R. G. Collingwood, *The Principles of Art*, p. 125.) To suppose that language is essentially a set of symbols like mathematics is to turn it into something unrealistically abstract.

Leaving language aside, then, I want to consider those symbols which we deliberately and consciously take to refer to something other than themselves. At one end of the spectrum there are objects which we may interpret according to a rule, but to which we could ascribe no meaning if we had not learned the rule. Such symbols, as for instance the flag flying at half-mast to signify a death, become, once we have learned them, as transparent as words. There is an arbitrariness about their meanings, just as it seems arbitrary that the word 'and', that vocable, should be used in English as it is, and that the word 'et' should have been so used in Latin. Any other sound would have done.

In contrast, there are true, full-blooded symbols which we seem able to interpret without rules, and without learning. To understand such symbolism seems to entail the use of imagination, imagination combined with thought, rather than thought alone, or the recollection of a lesson learned. We seem, here, to be moving along a continuum with the 'arbitrary' symbols or signs, which are transparent to us, at one end, signs whose meanings we read automatically once we have learned to do so, towards symbols which are 'natural', which speak to us not because their meanings have been learned, but because of something in their own intrinsic nature. This continuum may be thought of as running in parallel with that continuum of interpretation already suggested, which runs from necessary and automatic interpretation of perception at one end to the imaginative seeing of one thing 'as' another at the other end.

Natural symbols are akin to metaphors. Let us consider a
newly minted metaphor. Let us imagine the first time we read
the expression 'he lashed her with his tongue'. To lash is deliberately and aggressively, probably with excessive and only
partly controlled violence, to use a whip for punishment or
perhaps to cause an animal to wake up and move. We must
understand this meaning if we are to understand the metaphor
of 'lashing with the tongue'. We must be able to pick out the
relevant features of literal lashing and apply them to the situation of a verbal attack. We do this easily; we are not misled
into concentrating on the physical images of lashing, the nature
of the whip or the arm-movements of the aggressor. We go to
the heart of the matter and concentrate on his motives and on
the effects of his words on his victim. Indeed, we are so much
accustomed to translating the vocabulary of pain from the
physical to the mental that we have no clear way of drawing
a line between the two. Is there a metaphor, for example, in
the use of the word 'agony' for mental suffering? (or indeed in
the use of the word 'pain' itself?). If there is, it is a metaphor
that has almost lost its metaphorical 'feel'. The characteristic
of metaphor is that two applications of a word are understood
together. We do not lose the original meaning in the secondary
meaning; we see through the original to the secondary, and
the original meaning colours or illuminates the secondary. So
it is with symbols. A symbol is an object of awareness which
we see through, to that which it signifies, without losing the
sense of the object itself. But whereas when we use a metaphor
we are trying to throw light on a specific phenomenon, on
the effect of someone's words on his victim, for example, by
calling to our aid a better known, more obvious phenomenon
(and our metaphors are frequently derived from the visible
world and used to throw light on the world of mental events,
emotions, thoughts or characters for which we seem to have
no literal words to use), in our use of symbol we seem more
to be searching the visible for something we cannot exactly
specify.

The object for which we are searching may be referred to as
an idea. In Kant's terminology, a symbol is that which may
embody an aesthetic idea. Coleridge, in his usual somewhat
floundering way, and calling in aid Kant's German successors,

especially the idealist philosopher Schlegel, wrote of symbols as follows:

> I seem to myself to behold in the quiet object on which I am gazing more than an arbitrary illustration, more than a mere simile, the work of my own fancy. I feel an awe as if there were before my eyes the same power as that of reason which gives rise to ideas, the same power in a lower dignity, and therefore a symbol established in the truth of things. (*Statesman's Manual*, Appendix C)

It is in the previous appendix, however, that Coleridge most clearly related the understanding of symbols with the function of the secondary or creative imagination, as he himself had defined it in *Biographia Literaria* (see chapter 2). He there contrasts symbol with allegory. An allegory translates existing abstract notions into picture language, a language itself borrowed from objects of the senses. Thus Aesop's fables are allegories, since the 'moral' of the tale is thought of first (for example, that pride comes before a fall) and the animals who display the characteristics are nothing except manifestations of the vices or virtues intended. In the case of the symbolic, on the contrary, we start with a natural object, or perhaps an event, which is considered both for its own sake, as it actually is, and at the same time for the sake of something else we want to find in it. Coleridge says

> a symbol is characterized by a translucence of the special in the individual, of the general in the special, of the universal in the general: above all by the translucence of the eternal through and in the temporal. It always partakes of the reality which it renders intelligible; and while it enunciates the whole, abides itself as a living part in that unity of which it is representative.

Thus the symbol cannot be entirely separated from that which it symbolizes.

If we remember the way that Sartre described the honey from the spoon, sculpturing itself in a coil on the top of the honey in the jar, we can see that the honey not only itself exemplified the characteristics of viscosity or stickiness but stood for or signified the horrors of a cosmic viscosity of which, he alleged, we are naturally and inevitably afraid, this fear being a necessary part of our existence in the world. We cannot choose but to react to the sticky as we do: and thus honey or treacle is a natural symbol.

Sartre, as we have seen, did not want to ascribe such interpretation to the imagination, lest it should seem fanciful, far-fetched or merely personal. The dichotomy 'imagined/true' was still operative in his use of the terms. I have already suggested reasons for rejecting so narrow a concept of imagination. Coleridge's use of the concept of Secondary Imagination thus seems to me to be preferred, embodying as it does a central relation to understanding and truth. In Appendix B to *The Statesman's Manual* he continues thus: 'Imagination is that reconciling and mediating power which...organizing...the flux of the senses by the permanence and energies of the reason gives birth to a system of symbols harmonious in themselves and cosubstantial with the truths of which they are conductors.' The poet or artist of genius, as opposed to the talented fancy-monger, can 'give birth to' such symbols in his work, and because they are natural symbols, not 'far-fetched' outcomes of 'fancy', they will be understood by those who understand his work. Thus it is the function of the imagination to produce depth as well as clarity, and to make us aware of our own feelings, feelings of awe or fear or love, through the contemplation of the objects brought before us. It was such a capacity for combining depth with clarity that first impressed Coleridge when he met Wordsworth, and made him hail Wordsworth as a genius. The poetic genius, then, is able to discover truth through the treating of perceived forms (and we remember the ambiguity of Wordsworth's own use of the word 'form') as symbolic; and in so far as he is understood by his audience, their imaginations too work in this way, and they are enabled to see the timeless or eternal in the temporal.

The notebooks which Coleridge kept throughout much of his early life are full of his own experiments with symbolism, exact descriptions of actual objects of vision, through which he seems to be peering for a significance beyond the phenomena themselves. These jottings can be seen partly as *aides-mémoire*, for use or possible use in future poems, partly as the spontaneous record of intense feelings (often opium-induced) of love or awe or fear which he has felt momentarily as he looked at a natural object.

However, in addition to such searchings for significance, or for unity, there are many long entries in the notebooks which are, as it were, pure description, within which a primrose is simply a primrose and nothing else; and there are also long passages of scientific description. It was, as we have seen, the relation between such knowledge of the natural world and the knowledge of what lay behind it that fascinated the Romantics, Coleridge not least. He wondered at times whether too much exactitude of observation might not inhibit the imagination (*Notebooks*, ed. Kathleen Coburn, Pantheon Books, 1957, vol. 1, no. 1016): 'whether or no the too great definiteness of terms in any language may not consume too much of the idea-creating force in distinct clear full-made images and so prevent originality...original thought as opposed to positive thought'. But for the most part he was, it seems, convinced that the universal could be seen through the exactly perceived particular, just in the way that, later, Sartre was convinced of this.

I do not want to suggest that all symbolism is 'natural' symbolism. There are obviously objects used as symbols in a particular context, as part of a particular culture, where someone untaught, or ignorant of that culture, could not see the object as symbolic. Thus a crucifix is symbolic within the context of the Christian church, not otherwise. Yet although this is true, and although I have spoken of a continuum from an 'automatically' interpreted sign at one end and a full-blooded symbol at the other, it is possible, I believe, to draw a rough, though not an exact distinction, somewhere along this line between symbols which do awake our imagination, which convey what Kant called Aesthetic Ideas, and those which do not. Certainly, it is fairly easy to exclude a good many of the significant items at one end of the continuum. If we think of maps for example, they contain all kinds of different material which we can be taught to read, words, conventional signs, crude representations, (such as schematic pictures of bog-grass, windmills or castles) contour lines and so on. But nothing on the map is a symbol in the full-blooded sense. There is nothing there that is impregnated with meaning, that has the ambiguity demanded of full-blooded symbols. This ambiguity makes us think both of

the object itself and what we take it to mean. We cannot separate the meaning from the object. It is only when we have
learned the Christian story that we can see in the crucifix the
significance ascribed to it by Christianity. But once we have
been taught the story, then that significance and the form of
the cross itself are inevitably woven together. We can see more
in the visible object than meets the untaught eye.

Such interweaving of object and meaning is the work of the
imagination at its deepest and perhaps unconscious level. Writing of Trollope's use of river and torrent images for sexual
passion, Virginia Glendinning said this:

> It is no exaggeration to say that dozens of instances might be
> quoted where water and bridges over water are both the setting
> for and the substance of sexual crisis. Hoverings on the brink,
> leaps in the dark. The seasoned Trollope reader becomes con-
> ditioned to the strategy; the pulse quickens in anticipation. It
> is not useful to wonder whether the symbolism was deliberate.
> Symbolism is as old as language, and Anthony was skilled at
> transmitting subtextual messages. He was writing before Freud,
> a museum curator manqué, had prised apart the symbol and the
> symbolized and laid them out on display, side by side, separately
> labelled. Freud did art no special service by putting artificial
> membranes between layers of mind, and weakening the diffuse
> potency of sexual imagery by insisting on the naming of parts.
> (Victoria Glendinning, *Trollope*, Hutchinson, 1992, pp. 465–6)

We may notice that a symbol is ambiguous in another way.
In order to be interpreted it has to become an image or an idea,
a thought-imbued reflection, and hence in dualistic language
a 'mental entity'. Yet it is also an object, or form, in so far as
that is something in the physical world. And so the inner/
outer dichotomy must disintegrate when we think or see sym-
bolically. But we may still ask the question how, if I see more
in an object, a crucifix or an albatross or the arch of the sky
above my head, can I get you to see that 'more'; how can I get
someone else to experience what I take to be an illumination?
Whether such 'seeing more' can amount to understanding or
not depends largely, as one would expect, on whether what
is taken to be a symbol can be generally seen to be symbolic,
either immediately, or as a result (as in the case of the crucifix)

of explanation. And whether it can be seen as symbolic depends on whether the emotional colour of what is symbolized can actually be shared. The example of Trollope is illuminating: there is something 'natural' and readily grasped in the symbolism of rushing water, and the hovering on the brink; and he leads us to grasp its meaning by his manner of introducing it into his narrative.

On 14th April 1805, Coleridge made the following entry in his notebook:

> In looking at objects of nature while I am thinking, as at yonder moon, dim-glimmering through the dewy window panel, I seem rather to be seeking, as it were asking, a symbolic language for something within me that forever exists, than observing anything. Even when that latter is the case, yet still I have always an obscure feeling as if that new phaenomenon were the dim awakening of a forgotten or hidden truth of my inner nature. (Coleridge, *Notebooks*, vol. 2, no. 2546)

The truth Coleridge was searching for, and which he felt to exist already, to be discovered, was to be discovered by him, and not another; and it was in a sense a truth about him, his 'inner nature'. But the phenomenon which would reveal the truth was actually out there in the sky, and could be made to reveal its truth to others as well. And he must try to reveal it. For if revealed it would amount to a hidden truth, not about himself alone, but about others as well. John Stuart Mill, writing of Coleridge, said that the common accusation against 'transcendentalists' such as Coleridge was that 'they make imagination and not observation the criterion of truth...they lay down principles under which a man may enthrone his wildest dreams on the chair of philosophy, and impose them on mankind as the intuitions of pure reason' (*Essays on Bentham and Coleridge*, ed. F. R. Leavis, Chatto and Windus, 1971, p. 112). It can be only through the operation of some kind of common understanding of the the significance of natural phenomena that the proper employment of symbolism can be ensured, and the enthronement of the wildest dreams be avoided. It is, in fact, not simply a 'truth of *my* inner nature' that I seek in symbols, but a truth of *our* inner nature.

It is our similarities one to another that make sense of the appeal to 'our' inner nature. The way that the significance things have is shared is through sympathy, itself an aspect of imagination of the greatest importance to us. And it is only through sympathy that what is used as a symbol by one person can also be accepted as symbolic by another. But such acceptance is not always possible. Some imagery is too far-fetched, and we may gib at it.

If Sartre manages to persuade us not only that the viscous is threatening, but that somehow we always knew that it was, and that its threat defines and explains our position in the world and how we have always felt about it, then his interpretation of the symbolic honey may seem inevitable, and to afford a revelation not to be denied. And this is how he would like it to be. His writing, in *Being and Nothingness*, leading up to the image of the wasp drowning in honey, is emotive, rhetorical and deliberately manipulative of our imagination. It is perfectly possible for us to recognize this fact, see the point of this image, understand what Sartre is suggesting, and share the feeling temporarily, but nevertheless reject it if it claims to be the only possible way in which we can see ourselves in the world. It is plain that such a momentary grasp of meanings can be referred to as 'sympathy', while being less than full acceptance. It may be held that such emotional and partial acceptance is not suitable for philosophy, being more the intended outcome of novels or films: and many contemporaries, especially English-speaking philosophers, held that Sartre would have done better to stick to novel-writing or film-making. However that may be, what we have reached here is an indisputable connection between sympathy and the acceptance of an interpretation as intelligible, even believable. We need to pursue this connection further.

5

Stories

At the end of the last chapter, in which I was concerned with the symbolic, I established, as I hope, a link between sympathy and the general intelligibility of symbols. I want now to try to demonstrate that there are long-lasting, perhaps everlasting, areas of human sympathy which entitle us to claim understanding not only of the present, not only of symbols and metaphors, but of the past and the future as well. I shall argue that the intelligibility of these visions of present, past and future depends on what we may broadly refer to as values.

The word 'value' is a word from which we may immediately shy away. It sounds portentous; and it is much loved by politicians. We are told of Victorian Values, or Family Values. Yet it stands for a concept which is central to the understanding of both humans and other animals. It stands for that which those animals pursue and avoid, whether instinctively, because they are genetically programmed to do so, or because they have learned.

That to which we ascribe value, high or low, comprises everything that we believe to be good or bad, nice or nasty, pleasurable or painful, great or mean, and so forth. If there were no assurance of the permanence of such values (not only of the continuing ability of humans to make value-judgements, but of some continuity in the actual values they ascribe to things) then we could have no assurance of understanding the meanings people ascribe to things in the present, let alone in the past or the future. That we sometimes claim to do so rests on a conviction that, more or less, humans remain the same, intelligible to one another through their common likes and dislikes, and bound together by possible sympathy, throughout

time. That is to say we are aware of continuity through time
not merely in our own lives, but in the life of the human race
as a whole. We could not have such a concept of continuity
without imagination; for without imagination we could have
no idea of past, present and future. And the concept of continuity that we have is essentially linked to our continuing values.

One of the most important, indeed perhaps the central vehicle
for the conveying of such values, is the story. So C. S. Lewis,
in his essay, 'On Stories' (Lewis, *Of This and Other Worlds*,
ed. W. Hooper, Collins, 1982, pp. 25–45) argued that, for
example, the story of Jack the giant killer conveyed as its central
value, a kind of fear, the fear of the monstrous, which cannot
be expressed otherwise than in this kind of story, and which
is immediately intelligible. The narrative has a point, and this
point could not be made except by the idea of giants. It is not
that we actually fear giants, in real life; it is rather that we
know this kind of fear, a fear that we may experience, for
example, among some kinds of mountains – the Mountains of
Mourne in Lewis' experience. And we may be reminded of
Wordsworth in the Lake District, when, as a boy, he took a
boat and rowed out into the lake, as darkness began to fall:

> When from behind that craggy steep, till then
> The horizon's bound, a huge peak, black and huge
> As if with voluntary power instinct
> Upreared its head. I struck and struck again,
> And growing still in stature the grim shape
> Towered up between me and the stars, and still
> For so it seemed with purpose of its own
> And measured motion like a living thing
> Strode after me...
> (Wordsworth, *Prelude*, Book 1, 11376–85)

We recognize this particular kind of fear immediately, as children
do, in the story. It is the fear of giants.

To say that a story speaks of this, or any other intelligible
or recognizable value, must not be taken to imply that there
exist fixed entities, wholly separate from the ordinary world,
everlasting and unchanging, with names attached to them, which
are value-names. It is easy to see why an 'absolute' value, one

that, among its other attributes, must be capable of being recognized by everyone, must also be supposed to be unchanging.
For it might be thought that if it were not, it would not be
recognized again and again, at different times and by different
people. Thus, it could be argued that honesty, for example,
must be essentially the same wherever and whenever it is upheld
as a virtue, otherwise we could neither identify it nor name it,
and so could not intelligibly set it up as a moral ideal. Honesty
must exist, an eternal object of veneration. There is some truth
in this kind of argument. We certainly possess a general idea
of honesty, and we need this if we are to aspire to be honest,
or admire honesty when we encounter it in others. Some such
vague notion of what it means to be honest derives from our
acquired ability to use the word 'honest' in a way that can be
generally understood. But to say this is by no means to say that
the idea of the honest must be for ever fixed and immutable,
if it is to be the object of knowledge. We recognize honesty
only in particular and often widely differing manifestations of
it in others, or in particularly circumstanced aspirations in ourselves; and it is through these particular circumstances that we
add to, enrich or otherwise subtly change our idea of honesty.
Someone who is, as it were, creatively and imaginatively honest
(or generous or tactful, or sensitive as a violinist or a pho-
tographer) may be more important to our understanding than
our original vague idea, and may teach us, in a quite proper
sense, the meaning of what we value. That people can be thus
creative in their exemplification of a valued property does not
mean that they have a better knowledge of an immutable value
than we. It means that they have the imagination to work on
and develop what they value, in the course of their lives. We
have to think of such developments as real changes, yet so
related to the past that we can recognize them for what they
are.

What I mean may perhaps be illustrated with a musical
example. Suppose there is a Mozart symphony that someone
knows very well. Now he hears it for the first time played on
period instruments, by a small band with no conductor, led by
the first violin. The listener may feel that he had never really
heard the work before. Every note is distinguishable, every line
plays its part. A new dimension of clarity and understanding has

been added to his previous experience of this symphony. If he had not known the symphony already, the brilliant originality of this playing would not have struck him, or not with so much force. Yet, even with his new-found understanding, the listener may recognize that this is not the only, or the forever-perfect and unalterable interpretation. Other interpretations still have value; and the future may reveal yet more to enhance the understanding of the symphony (though obviously at the moment it is impossible to predict what form this enhancement may take). There is not just one performance that must for ever remain the pattern.

A belief in immutable values, existing somehow outside the world, though not unique to Plato and the Platonists, was certainly characteristic of them. Aristotle was severe with the Platonists for holding that values, especially the value 'goodness', had a separate, independent existence, or the word an unchangeable meaning. In the *Nicomachean Ethics* (Book I, ch. 6) he deployed a number of arguments against such a view, including the argument that knowledge of so unbending and fixed a universal would be useless. A weaver or a carpenter needs to know about what is good in weaving or carpentry, not about goodness in general. Even if one thinks of a less wide-ranging universal, such as health, it is useless if it is conceived as one single and undeviating pattern. A doctor certainly values health, Aristotle says; but he is interested in the health of men, even of the particular man who is his patient. 'It is, after all, individuals he is treating' (*NE* 1097a13). Aristotle also questions the intelligibility of speaking of such ideas as eternal, as if this somehow added to their value. 'A white thing which lasts a long time', he says briskly, 'is no whiter than that which perishes in a day' (*NE* 1096b4).

When Plato and his followers talked about Ideas or Forms, the Idea of the Good or the Beautiful, for example, they were certainly referring to what I have called values. And the main reason why they held that ideas must be eternal and unchanging, somehow outside time and therefore not subject to temporal change, was that if they were not they could not be known. Yet they must be known, or we could not recognize goodness or beauty when we saw them exemplified in the world. Plato's view (and this is a view that has been shared by many philosophers, including Descartes) was that the true model of knowledge was provided by mathematics. Numbers manifest properties and relations which are permanent and fixed: thus, once their properties are discovered and grasped, knowledge exists and cannot be denied, now or in the future. The mathematician is in permanent possession of what he has found to be true. In Greek, English and many other languages the words used for knowing and understanding are often metaphors derived from grasping, touching, holding, possessing. The desire for knowledge which is certain is the desire for a possession that cannot be taken away. Someone who knows the truth in this Platonic sense realizes, when he acquires the knowledge, that this is what he has in his possession. If he knows, he can't be wrong. In Plato's time, after all, geometry was in its infancy, and the satisfaction of Pythagorean and Euclidean proofs, indeed their intellectual beauty, was never far from his mind. It was against such a pattern that all knowledge and understanding must, he thought, be judged.

However, Plato believed that not everyone could become the possessor of true knowledge and understanding. A man must have a lengthy education before he could even approach it, and he must be born suitable for such education. At a lower level, he held that truths (or useful fiction) could be conveyed by myths, stories the point of which everyone could understand. Thus, he argued in the *Republic* that in the ideal state people should be taught to accept government, and learn to be content with the position in society which was appropriate to themselves, by being told the myth of the original distinction, in the distant past, between men of different 'metals', some intrinsically more valuable and finer than others (*Republic*, Book III, 415). That such stories were not themselves true did not alarm him. What they taught was true, the values they encapsulated were real values, and this was enough. He would have understood what C. S. Lewis said about Jack the giant killer, though he might have objected to the story, in that the value of the fearful was perhaps not one that he would have thought worthy of inculcation. He had no wish to see people revelling in or even exploring their own emotions. Plato himself used the device of myths in some of his dialogues, including the story of the cave in the *Republic*, and of the chariot and charioteer in the

Phaedrus, to suggest truth. But he regarded such narrative as an inferior way to learn; rational deductive argument is the highest, and only possible successful method, if we are to pursue truth.

For us, on the contrary, deductive argument is only one among many ways to approach the truth, and a way suitable only in certain fairly limited contexts. We have come to believe in the possibility of another quite different kind of knowledge and understanding, unthought of by Plato, and that is the historical. It is impossible to exaggerate the difference that the idea of history has made to our concept of understanding, and what a gulf this places between us and the Platonists. Before saying more about historical truth, however, I must digress to say a little more about story-telling in general. For plainly, though history is essentially a kind of narrative, not all narratives are historical. The aim of story-telling is to put a framework round the moment-by-moment flux of events so that they may be contemplated as displaying a pattern which makes sense. Human beings occupy an individual position not only in space but also in time. Both space and time constitute the point of view that each of us, inevitably, adopts. The 'I' who perceives occupies a world in which continuity with past and future is part of his perception, that part contributed by imagination. Thus, narrative is a natural mode of thought. The instinct to impose order on chaos is immensely important to us, and is an essential element in the control we can exercise over the world we live in. Nothing is so demoralizing or frightening as the feeling of slipping into purposeless confusion. (Anyone who doubts this should read an astonishingly vivid account of what it is like to be autistic, written by a highly educated autistic person, who suggests that what is missing in the child with autism is precisely the ability to categorize the impressions he has of the world, so that he can recognize the same thing when it recurs, and develop a sense of the continuity of things through time. For the autistic, everything is renewed every moment, in a kind of Hereclitan flux. The result is extremes of terror and confusion. (See 'Autism: A Personal Account', Therese Jolliffe et al., *Communication: The Journal of the Autistic Society*, vol. 26 (3), Dec. 1992, pp. 8–15.)

If we have a blackbird who sings outside our window, perhaps for several years in succession, it is almost impossible not to hear its song as a tune. We recognize it, identify it and re-identify it, perhaps become irritated by it because, not being originally constructed according to human aesthetic principles, it ends 'in the air' with no proper cadence. But it becomes a rememberable feature of life, in so far as we hear in it a re-identifiable shape. Without such a sense of order, intelligibility and memorability in our own lives we become helpless. We absolutely need plans and intentions by which to project into the future experience and principles derived from the past. The notion of ourselves as people, self-directed, motivated, respons-ible for what we do and say, able to assimilate and order even what happens to us by accident or apart from our own will, all this derives from our ability to interpret events according to a 'plot'. This does not mean rewriting history, but simply writing it, or telling it to ourselves without writing it down. Stories, then, are central to our ability to manage and under-stand the world.

Many of our most mundane explanations, our attempts to make other people understand what is going on, take the form of a story, with its beginning in the past and movement to the present. If, for example, you come upon me frantically grubbing about among the contents of the dustbin, and you ask what I am doing, I will make you see, as I hope, that my behaviour is not as irrational or pointless as it may seem, by embarking on a narrative. I tell you that I emptied the waste-paper basket this morning because it is dustbin day, and then later realized that I had thrown away an envelope with the address on it that I needed for answering the letter, and so on. All such narratives contain the concept of understandable human purposes and wishes. An immense amount of our discourse is in narrative form, whether we are attempting to explain what we are doing now in the light of the past and the future, or are trying to amuse, or gain sympathy or cut some kind of figure in our immediate company.

This is a far from original observation. Indeed, the idea of a story (or rather of Story) has lately become a familiar subject of scholarly, philosophical and theological writing. I hope I have suggested not only that stories are necessary, but that they are reconstructions of a kind essentially to involve imagination, which may interpret creatively both where its image-objects are

derived from memory, and where they are not. Yet to place
imagination so firmly in the centre of the creating of stories
has its hazards. For, as I have also suggested, we may seek the
truth through stories, and there remains a recurring tension
between imagination and truth. If it is by imagination that we
invent things through our narratives which we may please to
call truth, then it may seem that truth is nothing but fantasy,
the search for truth itself nothing but a fairy-story undertaking.
You may as well search for the crock of gold at the rainbow's
end. If we allow that everyone may tell a different story, constructing and ordering a different world, then it is hard indeed
to avoid the quagmire of total relativism, or the bog of what
may be roughly categorized as 'postmodernism'.

Let us consider, for example, one of many rather similar
books by Don Cupitt, the Cambridge theologian. In *What is
a Story?* (SCM, 1991) he argues that, whereas in the tradition
of Western Philosophy, starting from Plato, a story might be an
allegory, the vehicle (as we have seen above) for timeless and
unchanging truth, now we no longer believe in timeless truths.
We believe instead, he tells us, that truth constantly changes
with time, and so we can readily accept that truth is created
by story-telling. 'Another story, another truth.' He writes:

> Truth is no longer something out there; it is a way with words.
> The preacher, interpreter or artist is now making truth in the
> telling of the tale...The interpreter is no longer just a servant
> of the truth, but has become someone whose job is the endless
> production of truth. Truth is like music or love; it has to flow
> continually. Out of us, like living water. (p. 23)

And, even more rhetorically, 'So story structures time and the
world and keeps darkness and death at bay, at least for a
while. We are listening to Sheherazade again, putting off death
by listening to tales through the night. Narrative, only narrative
conquers darkness and the void' (p. 80).

Now what lies behind this is plainly a galloping and, I believe, in the long run destructive relativism. It is necessary to
keep our heads. The fact that we deploy the imagination in
constructing our picture of the real world and in making it
familiar to ourselves, and that those who suffer from delusions,

or who are autistic, are greatly disabled by not being able to
do this, should not lead us to suppose that we can construct
anything we like and call it reality. Indeed, the case of the deluded, who characteristically make false constructions, shows
that this is not so. Such wild relativism is, as I have said, the
hallmark of postmodernism.

'Postmodernism' is, literally, a term of art which has its
primary application in the visual arts. But it has been adopted
as well by literary critics, and is sometimes seen, not without
cause, to be a threat to intellectual analysis and the pursuit of
truth in all academic fields and beyond, in the world of culture
as a whole. It is a theory based on the belief that there can be
no such thing as a single, or even a properly privileged point
of view. The 'I' who was central to the Kantian theory, who
constructed the world of phenomena according to *a priori* laws
has, it is argued, had its day, along with the laws themselves.
Post-Kantian Romantics who sought to discover general truths
by examining themselves, their own lives and perceptions, were
pursuing a will-o'-the-wisp. There are those, moreover, who
suggest that radical relativism is the natural consequence of a
multicultural society. William Dunning, in 'Postmodernism and
the Construction of the Divisible Self', (*The British Journal of
Aesthetics*, April 1993, pp. 132–41) argues that 'the profusion
of alternative modes of thinking and consciousness' available
to us today makes it impossible to prefer one viewpoint to
another. All are equally possible to adopt.

Philosophically, such extreme relativism can be traced back
to Nietzsche (see, for example, Anthony Quinton's *A Cultural
Crisis*, University of St Andrews, 1992). The suggestion is
common among feminist writers, for example, that the attempt
to adopt or to impose a single point of view is the outcome
of a will to power. Thus, some postmodernist women painters
argue that to continue to use the traditional techniques of perspective, that is to represent the world from a single, 'privileged'
viewpoint is to try to impose a white male view on a shifting,
essentially multiple world, containing no stable elements, and
certainly no absolute facts or values.

There are, however, other opponents of the view that there
is such a goal as truth who are less political. They regard
truth-claims not so much as devices by which to dominate the

oppressed, as simply mistaken. Such a view is contained in Richard Rorty's attack on epistemology (Rorty, *Philosophy and the Mirror of Nature*, Blackwell, 1980), or, I suppose, in the works of Jacques Derrida, though it is hard to be sure exactly what he is saying, so deliberately obfuscating is his style. But it is fairly clear that he believes that there is no such thing as objective reality 'outside the text' (Derrida, *Speech and Phenomena*, Northwestern University Press, p. 54 and *passim*). It is Derrida's influence that can be most clearly identified in the remarks of Don Cupitt, quoted above, on stories. If there is nothing outside the text, then what the text says is a matter of little importance. Interpreting it is a kind of game, and endlessly telling stories a way of passing the time, a futility like that of the hapless Tony, condemned without apparent end to reading aloud to Mr Todd, at the conclusion of Evelyn Waugh's *A Handful of Dust*.

The notion of innumerable 'texts', stories invented either in the mistaken belief that they may be true, or else without any reference to the truth, but as an attempt at the manipulation of other people, and each, in any case, susceptible of infinite varieties of interpretation is, of course, intellectually depressing. For what could possibly be the motive for research, scientific or historical, if the goal of truth were removed from it? More than that, I believe that such relativism, if it were possible to sustain it, would have a positively harmful effect on our attitude to other humans. At first sight it might be supposed that the rejection of a single viewpoint, and the recognition of other equally valid points of view would be liberal, egalitarian and beneficially open. But, if it is seriously to be maintained that one viewpoint is literally as good as another, then this is the way to simple indifference. No one view is to be preferred, so who cares what anyone says or believes? 'They would say that wouldn't they?' Their vested interests are involved. So we can disregard whatever it is they say, with all-embracing cynicism.

We must somehow find a way to distinguish beliefs that are true and those that are either false or less explanatory, even though we know quite well both that people hold different beliefs from one another, and that in the course of history beliefs have changed. I quote from Anthony Quinton's lecture:

Much of what we now believe was not believed before. Much was believed that is now disbelieved. We may conclude that our own beliefs will be lavishly revised in the course of time... But that does not show that those of our beliefs that will be correctly abandoned in the future will be shown by that fact to have been only relatively true. What will be shown is that they were not true but only believed. And a great deal of what we believe has always been believed and always will be: that human beings feel pain, while stones do not; that water quenches fire; that apples are edible; that sea-water tastes salty. All beliefs are, indeed, first arrived at from a particular point of view. Often the falsity of a belief can be accounted for by some peculiarity of the point of view of the believer. But must the fact that all beliefs are in this way perspectival universally invalidate or relativise them? Are not some perspectives epistemically superior to others; daylight to darkness, calm to excitement, curiosity to anger? What is more if beliefs originate from a particular point of view, they are not locked into it. The believer can consider the matter from other perspectives and can incorporate the perspectives of others by critical interchange with them. (*A Cultural Crisis*, p. 34)

Now it is nothing but our knowledge (exemplified and realized in the whole of our life) that there exists shared human experience and shared human values that makes sense of our desire to tell the truth and be told the truth. This shared experience is the reality 'outside the text'. C. S. Lewis, writing of the Oedipus story, puts it thus:

Such stories produce a feeling of awe, coupled with a certain sort of bewilderment...we have just had set before the imagination something that has always baffled the intellect; we have seen how destiny and freewill can be combined, even how freewill can be the modus operandi of destiny. The story does what no theorem can quite do. It may not be 'like real life' in the superficial sense, but it sets before us an image of what reality may well be like at some more central region. ('On Stories', p. 39)

This is to say what Aristotle said when he compared poetry with history and judged that poetry was 'more philosophical'

(Aristotle, *Poetics*, 9, 1450b5), on the grounds that it dealt not with the particular but with the universal. We know that what we become aware of in the Oedipus myth is universal, because we know without doubt that humans have from time to time confronted such destiny-laden decisions. We know that we are not alone in our imaginative boat, and we are bound together in it by imagination and sympathy.

But we also know, better than Plato or Aristotle did, that we may seek truth not merely in myth but in actual history; and it is to this that I now return. The historian, though plainly concerned with particular events in the past, is attempting to present something timelessly true that his readers may grasp and understand at any time, now or in the future.

R. G. Collingwood, in his book *The Idea of History* (OUP, 1946, Partv), is concerned to distinguish the subject matter (and indeed the methods) of history not from those of myth or poetry, but from those of of the natural sciences. This he does by drawing a distinction between changes that have been brought about intentionally and those that have not. The natural sciences, he argues, certainly concern themselves with changes, but they are, for the most part, gradual and evolutionary. History, on the other hand, is concerned only with actions, and actions are the outcome of human thought or intention. History is thus, in an important sense, always the history of ideas. This distinction may well seem too simple: on the one hand, it seems plausible to argue that the subject matter of the natural sciences is not so much unintended changes in the world as human interpretation both of such changes and of unchanging features of the world; equally, it may be argued that events, not actions, often have enormous historical importance. Historians, not natural scientists alone, will doubtless in future years have to concern themselves with such natural changes as the thinning of the ozone layer, or accidents, which no one intended, such as the disaster at Chernobil. Nevertheless historians will, I believe, have to treat these matters as they affect humans; they will have to take into account the growth of human recognition of their own responsibility for such changes or accidents, and their consequent reaction to the changes themselves, that is to say the ideas that these events engendered. In so far as this is true, I broadly accept Collingwood's view that history is essentially the history of ideas.

The ideas which are the concern of history include intentions; they also include attitudes and value-judgements; and such attitudes and value-judgements are what lie behind the events recorded in documents, and what render intelligible the archeological remains of any civilization that we may discover. It is the grasping and understanding of such ideas that gives to history the same kind of 'timelessness' that belongs to the events and emotions described in novels and other forms of story. Collingwood himself put it thus:

> If [one] is justified in calling the right-angled triangle an eternal object, the same phrase is applicable to the Roman constitution and Augustus's deliberate modification of it. This is an eternal object because it can be apprehended by historical thought at any time; time makes no difference to it in this respect, just as it makes no difference to the triangle. The peculiarity which makes it historical is not the fact of its happening in time, but the fact of its becoming known to us by our rethinking the same thought which created the situation we are investigating and thus coming to understand that situation. (*The Idea of History*, p. 218)

He goes on: 'To the historian, the activities whose history he is studying are not spectacles to be watched, but experiences to be lived through in his own mind, they are objective or known to him only because they are also subjective, or experiences of his own.'

It may be tempting to dismiss this as mere rhetoric. But we should, I think, try to see what truth there is in it. As I have said, we are no longer inclined to restrict knowledge to knowledge of mathematical abstractions or other 'eternal' entities. In fact, we increasingly value knowledge of the world we live in now, not some other more permanent or changeless world which may be thought to lie behind or above it. Moreover, we are prepared to allow that there can be knowledge of thoughts and feelings, not just, for each of us, of our own inner life, but for all of us, of each other's as well as our own. To acquire such knowledge requires the imaginative understanding of what it is that humans value, and these are essentially shared values. To disseminate such knowledge when it seems to have been acquired may be the driving motive of the historian just as much as of the novelist or autobiographer. The truth in Collingwood's contention, then, is that in one sense the objects of historical research, the intentions people had and the values they embraced, though not 'unchanging' or 'eternal' like the objects of mathematics, are nevertheless 'timeless' (though attaching to a particular time in the past) just in so far as they are shared. When the historian or his readers believe that they have understood a series of events in the past, their understanding may consist, as Collingwood maintained, in the certainty that they have rethought or refelt what was thought or felt in the past. The past and the present thus become one, for there seems to be only one thought or feeling involved, and time becomes irrelevant.

The historian, however, has a unique and difficult interpretative task, and one of which, since the nineteenth century, we have become increasingly conscious. D. E. Nineham in an essay entitled 'New Testament Interpretation in an Historical Age' (Nineham, *Explorations in Theology*, SCM, 1977, pp. 145–65) explained what he meant by 'an historical age' in these words:

> Modern man is aware in a way that his predecessors have not been of the historically conditioned character of all human experience, speech and institutions. We are acutely aware that human life as lived in history is always life lived in the context of some particular cultural grouping. For every individual, no matter how original, what it means and feels like to be a human being and live a human life is to a large extent controlled by the presiding ideas of the cultural community to which it is his destiny to belong. (p. 148)

He goes on to quote T. E. Hulme:

> There are certain doctrines which for a particular period seem not doctrines, but inevitable categories of the human mind. Men do not look on them merely as correct opinion, for they have become so much part of the mind, and lie so far back, that they are never really conscious of them at all. They do not see them but other things through them...There are in each period certain doctrines, a denial of which is looked on by the men of

that period just as we might look on the assertion that two and two make five. It is these abstract things at the centre, these doctrines felt as facts which are the source of all the other material characteristics of a period.

If we seek to understand another time than our own, since we cannot have direct acquaintance with 'what it was like', but can come to it only through 'data', written, pictorial, musical or archeological, we must always attempt to see through these data to the categories and presumptions that are embedded in them, not given as opinions, but assumed either as facts or, we may properly add, indisputable values. And this is an extremely difficult thing to do.

To attempt such a use of historical data, that is to exercise a specifically historical imagination, is characteristic of twentieth-century professionalism, whether in the study of history itself, or in what we may call historical literary criticism and the history of science, philosophy or religion. To take one example, in the nineteenth century it was common, at least in the English-speaking world, to read and comment on classical authors as though they were somehow really adherents of Christianity, and would recognize more or less the Christian list of virtues and vices. Thus, for example, generations of Oxford undergraduates who had to read Aristotle's *Nicomachean Ethics* as part of the Greats course, would assume that Aristotle must have had the same concept of duty as they had been brought up to have, and they would therefore incorporate the word, most incongruously, into their translations of the text, where no such concept is to be found. Again, they would translate the Greek word 'ε'υδαιμονία' as 'happiness' and then proceed on the assumption that Aristotle used the same concept as they did. These are comparatively easy examples, where we can readily see an anachronistic idea being imposed on an ancient text, because the problems of translation from one language to another may point us in the direction of a slide from one set of values to another. But there are doubtless numerous examples of such slides within a single language, used over a long period of time.

In historical studies it was probably the great German historian, Mommsen, who, attempting to collect all surviving Roman inscriptions, began to look at them as revealing what it was like to be a legionary serving overseas under the Roman Empire, putting on one side as far as possible all presuppositions of his own time. He was thus exercising the specifically historical imagination in trying to read through the inscriptions, themselves conventional and non-literary texts, to an alien or at least long-distant culture. He did not have to 'remove the author' from his texts, in the manner of modern literary critics, for there was in a sense, no author to remove. But his method was, I suppose, to 'deconstruct' his material, and incorporate his findings in his history of the Empire. At any rate, it is certainly true that the greatest influence on classical studies in the last sixty years has been the influx into England and the USA of German scholars before the Second World War, who were the inheritors of the Mommsen tradition, and who taught us first and foremost to lay aside all our own assumptions, and thus begin to see how amazingly different the Greeks and Romans were from us. To read the data in this way is of course to exercise historical imagination. Without such efforts the claim to rethink the thoughts of the past is necessarily an idle boast.

Yet Collingwood, himself an ancient historian as well as a philosopher, who told us with some plausibility and great passion that this rethinking of past thoughts is what historians ought to do, never really addressed the central question: how do we know when we have succeeded? Let us suppose that we exercise our historical imagination to the very best of our ability, examining the data in as 'pure' and assumptionless a way as we can, asking our own questions of the texts as Collingwood would have us do. We come up with an interpretation of the story that, we say, 'makes sense'. We now, therefore, think we understand the story. Does this entitle us to make a claim to have discovered the truth? Does not the admitted fact that it was imagination that led us to the point we have reached count against such a claim?

Here we are confronted once again with the very question we had to address in considering the interpretation of symbols, and the telling and understanding of stories. At the end of the second chapter (p. 43), I argued that we may have to fall back, as both Hume and Coleridge did, on the concept of a 'genius' to help us answer the question. There is no doubt that there have been, and are, historians of genius who have so convinced us of their refusal to import inappropriate presumptions, who have so directly confronted the evidence, and told us what it means, that we cannot help believing that their imaginative reconstructions are true, and accepting them as truth. One of the most outstanding of such historians was Thucydides, outstanding partly because he was the first, of whom we know, to have been in our sense of the word a professional historian. He was, as he tells us, relying partly on eyewitness accounts for his account of the Peloponnesian war. Moreover, he had a grand design. He believed that the outcome, his History, and the insight he could provide into the causes of the events he recounted, and the intentions and passions that lay behind them would be, in his words, 'a possession for ever'. Yet this story, which we accept as truth, includes, we fully recognize, aspects of the History that are creations of Thucydides's imagination, and are signalled as such: I mean the great speeches, such as that of Pericles. These are not, and are not passed off as being, accurate, Hansard-like reports. Yet we accept them as conveying truth because they arise out of, and also illuminate, the historical situation we have come to understand. A great historian, then, can give us insight into how things were, because he is capable of sharing with us his own insight. He does this in great part by the depth and conviction of his own vision.

There is another aspect of equal importance. We trust Thucydides because he witnessed some of the events he recorded, and because he made plain his intention of presenting the facts, the course of events, as accurately as possible. Whatever the evidence the historian uses, whether he relies on memory or not, we cannot claim to learn the truth from him unless we have reason to believe that he has not in any way falsified the evidence, or used it over-selectively. To discover that this is so, we need as far as possible to compare his use of the historical data with other uses. (In this respect, Thucydides is perhaps atypical, since for much of what he writes about his History is the best, or the only, evidence we have. We therefore naturally succumb to him more totally than we would if there were more resources at our disposal.) In any case, the point can be seen that not just any story will enable us to claim that we have grasped the truth. As Collingwood himself well knew, the first task of the historian is to confront the data, and make of it what he can, honestly and impartially. This is the historian's duty. It remains true that we call that person a genius whose imagination we can trust, and to whose direction we willingly submit ourselves. In the case of the historian, his genius consists precisely in his power to see through the data to the truth that lies behind it.

Some historians have not been content to try to tell a story that is truthful, or imaginatively to reconstruct a small part of the past. Such historians have made grand claims not only to know the truth but to know the whole truth, and, in principle at least, to know the truth of the whole of history. This kind of claim derives in part, I suspect, from a lurking Platonism, according to which the only proper claims to knowledge are of fixed and unchanging universals. Thus, what could be known would have to be a kind of fixed design, within which the past could be seen to have unfolded according to necessary laws, and which could be grasped as itself a kind of changeless pattern.

In this connection, it is worthwhile briefly to consider the way that Sartre, in his later writing, was caught up in the conflict, for such it must necessarily seem, between universal Truth and particular truths of history. He developed, almost, it seems, against his better judgement, a concept of what he called the True History, according to whose laws one could understand, not just what particular event occurred, but how it connected with other events, by a kind of inner necessity. Such is, in general, the 'absolutist' claim. After the Second World War, Sartre realized that he must involve himself with politics, and that his romantic individual-centred existentialism gave him literally no outlet into political reality. Believing that the political future lay with Marxism, he was accordingly determined to marry Marxism to existentialism, or, more accurately, to accept Marxism, and show how existentialism could be used to illuminate and humanize it. All this he sketched in *The Problem of Method*, first published in 1957, and in altered form standing as a preface to *The Critique of Dialectical Reason* (J.-P. Sartre, *Critique de la Raison dialectique*, Gallimard, 1960). Sartre held that, though Marxist materialism was an eternal and unchangeable truth, yet the dialectic of history could not be understood save from within the consciousness of individual humans whose particular actions at a particular time and place were what actually carried history forward. Individuals form intentions and projects; they alone look forward, decide and plan. An awareness of the past and the future of each individual goes into the making of his projects. Yet, accepting Marxist materialism, Sartre held that individuals were the outcome of their own economic place and time; but they exemplified this economic situation in their own deliberate acts, whether separately or in groups. Thus, if one could, with infinite and painstaking accumulation of detail, construct the biography of an individual, conveying exactly the conditions in which he was born and brought up, how he reacted to these conditions, and how the grasp of them motivated the actions of his life, what he thought and what he wrote, then this would tell the whole story of history, for in principle it could be interlocked with all other biographies, necessarily. Seeing the world from the point of view of an individual would show, though it would not explicitly state, the nature of the historical pattern. Sartre attempted such all-embracing biographies, notably in his life of Flaubert, which, unsurprisingly, he never finished. It is within that book that the tension became most apparent between two views of history. On the one hand it was a grand design, to be discovered and recorded once and for all, one and the same for ever; on the other hand it was an imaginative reconstruction, an explanation given by one person, and conveying truth, if at all, through an individual imaginative insight into the mind of another, an exercise in 'thinking his thoughts'. Sartre claimed that in principle a biography could communicate everything, and this because the life of one man contained within itself the necessary dialectic of history as a whole. In a 1971 interview, Sartre said:

> I would like [the Life of Flaubert] to be read with the idea in mind that it is true, that it is a true novel. Throughout the book Flaubert is presented as I imagine him to have been, but since I used what I think were rigorous methods, this should also be Flaubert as he really is, as he really was. At each moment in this study, I had to use my imagination. (*Sartre in the Seventies*, André Deutsch, 1978, p. 123)

The 'rigorous methods' are the methods of the dialectic, the discernment of the one single pattern in history. What Sartre would have been unwilling to admit was that this too was discerned, if it was, only by the imposition of an imagined framework, a conception of a one true history or science of man, which he saw in the historical data before him. Both as a novelist and biographer, and as a dogmatic Marxist historian, he was exercising his creative imagination by imposing a pattern on raw material. In the end, as it happens, he is more likely to carry us with him by the power of his novelist's rather than his Marxist's imagination. After all it is with the details of another human being's life that we can best exercise our own imaginative sympathy.

Where we do accept an imaginative construction, and believe ourselves to be thinking the thoughts of Flaubert, or any other historical character, we suppose ourselves to have reached understanding. This is the point of reading history, and to produce such understanding is the historian's aim in writing it. We can have confidence in the historian if he can make us understand the intentions, the motives, the projects, the fears and wishes of his characters, whether or not he believes in any 'grand design'. This is the outcome of Sartre's attempt to marry the individualism of existentialist philosophy, within which each human designs his own life, with the impersonality of Marxist theory: in the end the theoretical design is irrelevant to the truth of the historical account.

If this is so, the imagination is shown to be engaged in the reading of history in exactly the same way as it is engaged in the reading of novels or of autobiography. The way we come at understanding, or the truth, is different in each case; the kind of material we are presented with to show us the truth has been differently assembled. But in each case we are unable to accept what we are presented with as truth, unless it contains shared and intelligible values.

Of course the historian must always present his narrative from a certain point of view (and this in itself makes the Marxist concept of One True History suspect); and it may be thought that this will lead us into a kind of historical relativism no less worrying than total moral or scientific relativism. There could be as many true historical accounts of the past as there were people in the world. The past would then seem to slip out of our grasp altogether. But just as some interpretations of the natural world seem bizarre and unacceptable, and some moral interpretations ill-based or self-interested, and so not really moral at all, so there can be dotty or incongruous interpretations of the past, or interpretations which fail to explain, or fly in the face of the rest of what we know about the world. We will never come to the belief that we are thinking the thoughts of people in the past unless we keep our feet on the ground. All the time in seeking to reach historical understanding, we are seeking to understand 'us', that is, humans in the world. Sometimes we are therefore in a position to say 'We cannot accept that'; 'It is too implausible'; 'It is too far-fetched'. This is not to say that there is one right interpretation, any more than there is one correct value, or even one self-consistent set of values. 'We', humans in the world, change and perhaps develop, and so our understanding changes and develops. Nevertheless, we have to pay regard to what we may call common sense as the basis of knowledge. Our interpretations of the past may change, as we learn more about certain aspects of the world, about human psychology or genetics, the function of the human immune system, or the structure of matter. But there could be some accounts of past events which we could never accept, whatever new sophistication we acquired. Let us imagine that someone is attempting to explain the logistics of a seventeenth-century battle, when, perhaps, a contingent of horse appeared on the scene, bringing reinforcements or supplies, with what appears incredible speed. We will not and cannot accept, as an explanation of the speed, that the horses flew to the scene. We know, have always known, and will always know that horses cannot fly, and that the aeroplane which might have flown them did not exist in the seventeenth century.

We should also bear in mind that although historical knowledge can, in principle, be acquired, yet in any particular case we may have to regard knowledge as an ideal to be approached, not as something we can ever claim with certainty to have achieved. Very frequently, the most we can say is that, in interpreting the past, we aspire to the truth, though at the same time knowing we shall not reach it. But this is more to do with the complexity of events, or perhaps the paucity of evidence, than with the numbers of different points of view we may adopt. Some points of view are untenable. If we hold that a text can be read in any way whatever, then it becomes futile to read it; it will tell us nothing of interest. Not just any story will do in history, any more than it will in science.

All the same, though I have argued that plausibility has its limits, it may be objected that I am guilty of the absurdity of suggesting that there is no substantial difference between history and fiction, since what we use to give sense to each is the same, the constructive and sympathetic imagination. But of course this is far from true. History is not just another story, with a beginning, a middle and an end. It is, on the contrary, a story with no end. We are in the middle of it; and whatever it cannot tell us, it can tell us something of how we got to be where we are. The function of imagination is to think about what is not in front of our eyes, and this includes thinking about non-existent things, like Emma and Mr Knightley, about future things which do not yet exist, and about past events which cannot be literally recovered. This last is history. But between those historical things and us there is an all-important link of continuity. It is not only values and sensibilities that are enduring, it is actual objects as well. If we walk round a garden, or through a forest, or if we climb the tower of a cathedral or attend a service in it, we are engaged with objects that have persisted through time, and which affect our own lives now. This is the vast difference between history and fiction. I have spoken about the essential publicity of values, the fact that 'we', humans, can sympathize with each other's wants and needs, fears and hatreds. We can therefore understand our own history. And because history has no denouement, because it is not yet finished, it is a matter of great importance to enable the next generation of humans to go on with the story as they choose, to understand the story so far, and contribute to the construction of the next chapter. So the difference between history and fiction is essentially a practical one, in that it determines not only how we think about the past but how we, the human race, will conduct ourselves in the future. The past, as presented in history, is not over and done with.

6

Personal Identity

In this and the following chapter I shall be concerned with a particular branch of history, namely autobiography. It is in autobiography that the connection between our imagination, our values and our awareness of time is most clearly to be seen. But in order to bring out these connections, it is necessary first to consider memory, upon which, obviously, the existence of autobiography as a separate literary form depends. I shall therefore postpone the discussion of that form until the next chapter. The concept of memory has long been central, not only to the philosophy of mind in general, but especially to the philosophy of personal identity. The notion of personal identity is that upon which the very possibility of autobiography rests. And so we must first look at this personal identity itself.

What is it that we assume about ourselves, when we take it for granted without question that each of us is a person who, if he so chooses, can tell the story of his life? We are dealing here with ideas that are seldom examined except by philosophers, but which lie at the root of all our ordinary common-sense thoughts about ourselves. And so, in raising this kind of question (and this is a quite general point), we must take care not to stray too far from common sense. After all, if we are looking at presuppositions, these must relate to, and be partially expressed in, ordinary modes of thought. It would be of no interest to come up with a concept of an 'individual' or a 'person' which bore no relation to our practical concerns, or our beliefs about ourselves and other people. In an interview with P. F. Strawson, published in the magazine *Cogito* in spring 1989, Dr Pivcevic asked him about his book, *Individuals*, and said that in it Strawson had 'come down on the side of common sense'. And he asked, 'Why, as philosophers, should we trust common sense?' to which Strawson replied as follows:

> I wasn't concerned to defend common sense as such. I was concerned rather to elucidate the general structure of our conceptual scheme, i.e. the most general structural features of our thought and talk about the world and ourselves. This work of conceptual elucidation seems to me the essential philosophical task. The aim is to achieve a kind of reflective conceptual self-consciousness.

To try to 'elucidate the general structure of our conceptual scheme' is to return to the tradition of Kant. It is such 'conceptual self-consciousness' that we need to pursue in exploring the twin notions of memory and personal identity; and we must start from where we are.

I have treated these topics at greater length elsewhere (see *Memory*, Faber and Faber, 1987). However, I make little apology for discussing them again because I have to some extent rethought the issues since 1987 (without much changing my general views on them) and have been fortunate enough, since the book appeared, to engage in discussion with some philosophers and scientists, on whose views (I hope not too much misrepresented) I rely heavily in what follows. I suppose that no one would deny that our memory, while indissolubly involved in our present perceptions, that is in the manner in which we perceive and interpret our perceptions, is also linked, with equal strength, to our emotions. Memory can give rise to deep feelings of joy, or of remorse or regret or simple nostalgia. And so we tend to think of memory, like those emotions themselves, as part of that mental or psychological aspect that gives our human life itself its particular and individual colour. Yet it would be completely wrong to place memory on one side of the Cartesian mind/body distinction, or, for that matter, of a psychological/physiological divide. Indeed, as should already have become clear, it is my contention that such dichotomies, though we may naturally tend to fall into them, are profoundly misleading; and thinking about memory may perhaps bring out more clearly the mistake that the sharp division between the mind and the body, the inner and the outer, contains.

It seems that the capacity to remember is essential to the identity of all animals, not just of humans. It is this fact that makes memory so fundamental a faculty for those attempting to explain how we think of human individuals. It is central to the lives of even our remotest biological ancestors. We need not, and should not, ascribe virtues to other animals, nor intentions, nor regrets, nor aspirations. But we cannot but ascribe memory to them. We know quite well that we can teach our dog tricks; that parrots can make sounds, the sounds of human speech, by practice, that horses remember at a particular place that some terrifying experience befell them in the past; that rats remember the way through the maze to where the food is placed. Even octopuses, we know, can remember what to seek and what to avoid. Every animal, however lowly by our scale of valuation, organizes its life in accordance with its memories.

It may be objected that all reference to other animals is irrelevant. For the kind of memory associated with the idea of human identity is quite different from any memory that animals other than humans may exhibit. It is true that whereas in talking about, say, imagination or mathematical prowess, we realize that we are dealing with things specifically human, while in talking about memory we may be led into thinking about the extent to which dogs or flatworms or indeed computers have 'memories', nevertheless, so this argument goes, there is a kind of conscious memory, a way of knowing that a thought is a memory and refers to the past, which is unique to humans, and which is quite removed from that which has sometimes been referred to as 'habit' memory and which other animals share. In thinking of the connections between human identity and memory, surely we should concentrate on this 'conscious' memory, or recollection, not on that kind of memory common to humans and other animals? I believe that this objection is based on a mistake. It suggests that while there may be some kinds of memory which are part of any animal's life, there is a more interesting or elevated kind of memory, conscious memory, or memory of something specifically allocated to the past, which is purely mental, which belongs to the inner life of humans and of them alone, and which is a matter of thoughts, images and, perhaps, meanings.

It is necessary to take seriously this objection and the thought that is behind it, for it lies at the heart of the kind of dualism that I am concerned to argue against. I want to suggest that there are not two distinct kinds of memory; but rather that memory, being essential to any individual animal of whatever species, may develop in the course of evolution into something more sophisticated, as animals themselves develop. What we are talking about is physiology or morphology; and physiology, unlike physics, is an essentially historical subject. It is concerned both with the growth of species one out of the other, and, within a particular species, with the way an individual animal matures and develops.

Learning from the past rests on the ability to recognize *kinds* of things, that is to say it entails an ability to pick out features of a situation and think of them as able to recur. This ability is the same as that which enables men or other animals to treat certain features of their environment as significant, for it is only in so far as they may possibly recur that they are identified, and become the object of emotional reaction, taken to mean something for the future. It is to possibly recurring things that values attach. Thus, a nervous horse may see features as significantly recurring in circumstances not identical with the first circumstances in which it was frightened. If it has once been frightened by having to enter a horse-box it does not require that there should be the same box in the same place for it to be frightened again. If the horse had language, it would say to itself something like 'it's one of those again'.

What the horse experiences, in this example, could be described as a kind of cognitive recognition, though without benefit of language. It has been argued by, for example, Richard Gregory (see his *Mind in Science*, Weidenfeld and Nicolson, 1981), that cognitive recognition or recall could not occur without language. But this must surely be wrong. For we are perfectly prepared to allow that infants may recall things before they can speak. It is not speech, but selection or recognition of features that is required for memory. Gerald Edelman has sought to put such selection into a wider biological context (see, especially, Edelman's *Bright Air, Brilliant Fire*, Harper-Collins Basic Books, 1992). He argues that there are systems of selective adaptation which are not cognitive at all. His example is that of the immune system, and he suggests that it is possible to describe the brain as an analogous system. The importance of such a model of the brain is that it does not require that information should be fed from somewhere into a pre-existing fixed system. Rather as antibodies are formed, even when quite unexpected and new viruses enter the body, if the immune system is working properly, and the system thus changes itself, so the system that is the brain itself develops ways of adapting to new events. The key concepts here are those of selectivity and adaptation. Just as, over an evolutionary time-span, different species develop selectively to adapt to and fit their environment, so within the life of any particular animal, its brain develops, and its behaviour changes in accordance with unforeseen variations in its environment, selected as significant. The connection between the evolution of the species and the development of the individual is this: the constraints which limit the behaviour of individual animals are set by the value systems that a species of animal has, given it by evolutionary selection, and passed on genetically from one generation of animal to another. Thus, the horse has, through evolutionary time, become the kind of animal that may, for example, be excited by the hunting horn, or frightened by the cavernous entrance to the horse-box. And thus an individual horse will exhibit suitable excitement or fear by selecting responses to situations, even new situations, rather as antibodies are formed on the entry to the system of molecules of a particular shape. The living organism adapts to new situations, in accordance with the overall adaptation of the species of which the animal is a member. And so each animal, even within one species, has its own selective and adaptational system, depending on what actually happens to it during its life. The complexity of the brain is such that no two members of a species will behave in identically the same way, and as the history of each varies, so its memory and its recognition of things will vary, individually. It is not, I believe, too fanciful to find a parallel here between the evolutionary theory of the brain propounded by Edelman, and Kant's system of necessary, or *a priori* psychology. For it cannot be denied that Kant started from a psychological viewpoint. How did perception, viewed as a mental, internal phenomenon actually work for humans? How did it (how could it) bring them to possession of that scientific knowledge which they undoubtedly had? How did it cause them to be aware of themselves as observers? According to Kant's theory, there are functions of the *a priori* imagination which, as we have seen, are shared by all rational creatures, and are fixed and unalterable; they determine the application of the categories in the light of which we parcel up the world to make it intelligible and predictable. There is also, for each rational creature, an empirical imagination which will vary from one individual to another, according to what he has actually experienced in the course of his life. For each, it will be different from all others. In Darwinian terms, this is equivalent to the distinction between what belongs to the species as a whole, as a result of its evolution, and what is unique to each individual member of the species. This may be no more than an analogy; but that the analogy works may be a guide to the truth.

Now if an animal learns it must be said to possess memory. And if, by learning, it changes its behaviour this will be because, having categorized and remembered, the values which it already has are engaged. For values, what is to be sought or avoided, are an intrinsic part of the categorizing an animal does. A dog will do its tricks in the expectation of reward, that is, something it likes or values. The horse will refuse to enter the box because of its hatred of confined and dark spaces. It can be induced to do so by the emerging of other values, a hay-bag in sight, or a familiar, soothing groom. The value systems of any animal are centred in those structures of the brain such as the hypothalamus which have evolved according to the demands of the survival of the species. They are common to the species.

In contrast, if information is fed into a computer and stored, though this information may be combined with other information in numerous different ways, it will not itself change. The categories within which the information is parcelled up will remain constant. But in the case of animals, because the kinds of categories developed by an animal brain are not fixed, but are subject to evolutionary change over time, memory will involve constant and gradual recategorization. Memory entails constant rehearsal in different contexts of what was the original categorizing system. (We may, for example, require our dog to perform its tricks in all sorts of different circumstances.) Thus memory, unlike the information system of the computer, is inexact, but capable of spreading, becoming more general, linking with other parts of the mapping or plotting-out system of the brain. There is a dynamism in animal memory lacking in the memory of a computer. The inexactitude and variability of memory are based on the fact that categorization itself is inexact. The world does not come to us, or to any other animal, already packaged up into 'things'. Yet it is only by the recognition of 'things' that we can manage the world. To quote Professor Weiskranz (*Categorization, Cleverness and Consciousness*, OUP, 1985, p. 3) 'the recognition of objects is the first prerequisite for the survival of an animal.' To some extent the animal makes objects for itself.

Generally speaking, we are quite happy to say of an animal, whether our nervous horse or a particular goldfinch in a flock of goldfinches, that what makes it an individual, one animal or one bird persisting through time, is that it is a particular body. True, it is very difficult to identify and re-identify a goldfinch as one and the same bird. But we know that it would be possible to do it if, for example, we ringed it, or if we kept it in a cage, for ever under our eye. The reason we know it would be possible is that we know that this goldfinch emerged from one particular egg, and will live out its own life, not any other bird's, till it dies. But after our glance at the functioning of the brains of animals, we are now in a position to say a little more. It is not simply the observable body of the animal which distinguishes it from all others of its species; it is also that part of its body which we cannot see by ordinary means, its brain, which is unique to itself, and makes it the individual it is. It, the animal's brain, has its own development and its own history, depending on the unpredictable growth-pattern of that animal as an embryo, and the circumstances it has encountered then and at a later stage. One goldfinch is different from all the others in the flock. It is still more obvious that this is the case with the horse. Our horse has a system of memories not shared by other horses, and this system affects the way it categorizes and recategorizes things in its world. Experiences re-enter its perceptual system in a manner unique to it, and not wholly determined by its genetic inheritance. The brain of our horse actually changes and develops over time so that it becomes different from other horses, not simply as any spatial object differs from another, but structurally. If this is right, then it seems plain that what we can say of goldfinches and horses we can also say of humans.

Yet it may still be objected that I have missed the point. I have spoken, it is true, of categorization and of memory. But I have not said anything about the abilities of the human brain that go beyond these functions. What about the formation of abstract ideas (including the ideas of past, present and future)? Above all, what about consciousness? Is not this the extraordinary mystery of the human brain which makes it totally different from the brains of any other animals? And is it not therefore this consciousness which distinguishes human from other memory?

The developmental theory of the brain entails that nothing absolutely new is needed to account for its ability, in the human, to form concepts, nor for the phenomenon of consciousness itself (see Edelman's *Bright Air, Brilliant Fire*, pp. 113–20). As the frontal cortex of the brain evolved, so the ability grew not merely to receive more and more stimuli and remember them, but, without new stimuli, to rethink what had gone before and generalize it. Higher-order maps could be made of the first-order maps of brain connections. The brain became capable of passing comment on its own activity. And from concepts grew language, and from language consciousness. We may divide consciousness into two, primary and higher. Animals with primary consciousness are aware of the present scene that they occupy, and moreover this present scene is imbued with the categories and the memory they have developed, and the values they have attached to them. Their consciousness is, however, like a beam of light which is shone into a dark room. It illuminates what there is, without illuminating what falls outside the beam. It is clear from behavioural tests that many animals other than humans possess such consciousness; and that humans suffering some kinds of brain damage have this kind of consciousness and this alone. Studies by Weiskranz on rats and Oliver Sacks on brain-damaged humans are among the many studies that confirm this. Higher consciousness, on the other hand, is, it seems, co-existent with the growth of language, in evolutionary terms, and involves not merely the past-imbued present, the narrow beam of illumination of primary consciousness, but the idea of the past and the future, and hence a notion of the self as someone who is continuous, then, now and in the future. We can observe the growth of such consciousness in individual children; and we can presume that in the course of evolution the human brain developed the morphology to make such consciousness possible, more or less at the time when the rest of the body, the larynx and the epiglottis and the so-called oral cavity, which are unique to man, also developed to make speech possible. With the growth of language, humans could begin to refer to themselves, and also to try to describe, by the systematic use of words or other symbols, how things seemed to them, what they actually experienced from within. These developments were all based securely on those powers of memory and categorization of the world that all animals share.

Such neurological theories of meaning and of the development of consciousness are empirical, in that experimental work now proceeding is capable of supporting or, of course, disproving them. Such work involves the modelling of various functions of the brain by means of computers (one must distinguish between the use of computers to replicate certain functions of the brain, and the suggestion that the brain is to be explained as if it were itself a computer. I shall consider such theories in a moment). It also involves the observation of animal behaviour, and the observation of human cases of differing kinds of brain damage. There are those who object to any such theory on the grounds that it cannot be properly scientific. Such objectors regard a theory based, even in part, on reports from patients, or on that most distrusted source, the introspection of language-using scientists, as irremediably flawed and 'subjective'. And it is true that almost any attempt to account for human consciousness will necessarily involve the 'common-sense' observations of scientists and others who are conscious. This has always been true of philosophers concerned with the mind; Aristotle, Hume, Ryle and Wittgenstein to mention only a few. Nevertheless, such reports can be correlated both with human and animal actions and, these days, with observation of brain structures and functions. The great merit of such a theory as this, however, is that it takes biology seriously. It does not attempt to reduce the brain to a series of physical regularities. This is of the utmost importance.

The philosopher Daniel Dennett may serve as an example of those who use the ideas of Artificial Intelligence to try to explain the nature of the brain in physical terms. It is not part of my purpose to enter in any detail into his arguments. He himself recognizes that it may be hard to reconcile people to the belief that the brain is a computer, or that a computer could be constructed which would fully replicate the human brain; and one of his best-known articles is entitled 'Why you can't make a computer that feels pain' (D. C. Dennett, *Brainstorms*, Harvester Press, 1978, pp. 190–223). Yet the desire to perform such a feat is very strong. For there is a sense in which physical reductionism is uniquely satisfactory. Physics is the most fundamental and the most far-reaching of the sciences. It is nothing new to wish to show that everything can in the end be understood in its terms. To reach such a position sometimes seems the ultimate goal of the sciences, and thus of understanding, even if, on a day-to-day, common-sense level we could not make much use of such understanding. However, what makes it difficult for people fully to accept physical reductionism is the sense they have that when, as conscious beings, they refer to themselves in the first person, ascribing thoughts, feelings and insights to themselves rather than another, they are referring to a central 'self', the recipient of all stimuli, and the initiator of their own thoughts and actions. Literature is full of records of a grasped consciousness of self, often coming suddenly and unheralded to children, who remember thinking 'I am I. No one can ever take that away from me'. Anthony Powell, for example, records such a sudden realization in the first volume of his autobiography (he was five or six years old at the time):

> After the park and the street, the interior of the building seemed very silent. A long beam of sunlight, in which small particles of dust swam about, slanted through the upper window on the staircase, and struck the opaque glass panels of the door. On several occasions recently I had been conscious of approaching the brink of some discovery; an awareness that nearly became manifest and then withdrew. Now the truth came flooding in with the dust-infested sunlight. There was no doubt about it. I was me. (*Infants of the Spring*, Heinemann, 1976, p. 46)

But of course such awareness need not be sudden; it may come gradually to permeate our perception, our decisions, our expressed likes and dislikes. We may call such groups of thoughts, feelings and beliefs the belief in a persisting self. Descartes' 'Cogito ergo Sum' was a philosophical account of such a belief, and it led him to the conclusion that the inner and the outer, the mental and the physical, were two wholly distinct substances, joined it is true in the case of a human by the pineal gland at the base of the brain, but distinct nevertheless, and different in kind one from the other. No reductionism was logically possible, according to his theory.

Descartes' conclusion was a matter of argument, not of experience. David Hume, attempting a wholly empirical account of our knowledge of ourselves in relation to the external world, concluded that all we have from experience, as opposed to anything that we may construct or imagine, is a series of sense impressions, and that we are not and cannot be, in addition, aware of a self who 'has' these impressions. Impressions, of hot, red, pain, pleasure, anger, love, simply come one after another, in a perpetual series. Any thoughts or ideas we may have are necessarily derived from these impressions. And since we have no impression of the self at the centre, we can have no idea of such a self either. Impressions are all of them impressions of something else. Hume says in the *Treatise* (Bk I, Pt IV, sec. VI, pp. 251–2) 'If any impression gives rise to the idea of self, that impression must continue invariably the same thro' the whole course of our lives; since self is supposed to exist after that manner. But there is no impression constant and invariable.' And he goes on:

> For my part, when I enter most intimately into what I call myself, I always stumble on some particular perception or other...I never can catch myself at any time without a perception, and never can observe anything but a perception... The mind is a kind of theatre, where several perceptions successively make their appearance; pass, repass, glide away and mingle in an infinite variety of postures and situations. There is properly no simplicity in it at one time, nor identity in different; whatever natural propensity we may have to imagine that simplicity and identity. The comparison of the theatre must not

mislead us. They are the successive perceptions only that constitute the mind, nor have we the most distant notion of the
place where these scenes are represented nor of the materials of
which it is composed.

But, for most of us, Hume seems to have missed our central
presumption; there is an 'I' who perceives. And it is this thought
which makes people so unwilling to accept reductionism.

To return to the reductionist Dennett: he allows virtually
no theoretical limit to the extent to which we could make a
computer which was in every way the equivalent of a human
mind (or presumably of the mind of a rat or a monkey). And
in this he is aware of his alliance with David Hume. According
to Dennett, Hume could find no impression of the self because
such a thing is unnecessary for a mind to function as our minds
do. In a conversation with Jonathan Miller, broadcast in 1983
on BBC television (Jonathan Miller, *States of Mind*, BBC, 1984,
pp. 68–81), Dennett explained that the science of Artificial Intelligence models the functions of the brain by sub-dividing those
functions into specialist functions, which when put together can
produce all the results that the human mind can produce, the
mind itself thus being seen as a complex set of physical systems.
He gives an example:

> Take a chess-playing computer. We first break that down into
> a number of experts. We have a move-generator, a bright-ideas
> person; and then we have a move-critic who will criticize the
> moves generated by the move-generator; and then we have a
> referee who makes sure that the rules are being obeyed; and then
> we have a time-keeper who makes sure that nobody spends too
> much time on any one job. Then if you focus on the move-critic,
> who has just some of the information, and look at him more
> closely, you see that he's broken down into a team of smaller
> stupider sub-critics, petty clerks each doing a little job. You get
> specialists, and, as we all know, specialists know more and
> more about less and less. And these in fact know not very much
> about very little. But put them together into large armies, and
> a whole system of these stupid elements can exhibit behaviour
> which looks distinctly intelligent, distinctly human.

The point of this image is to demonstrate that information comes into the mind and is processed piecemeal, just as Hume thought; and that nothing else is needed save the system itself to make this into something that works as we know that the mind does work, to solve problems, intervene in the world, make theories about it and put those theories to further use. Dennett goes on:

> There's a strong inclination when one starts developing models of this sort to exempt the self, and say 'maybe I do have all of these little sub-systems in me, but then there's the king sub-system, the boss; there's the one at the centre who knows it all and controls the others and that's the really wonderful and mysterious one. That's the seat of the soul.' But I think it's a bad mistake.

Let us think a bit further about the chess-playing computer, or chess-playing robot (for we do not need to add much to the idea of a mathematical computer coming up with solutions to problems to make it into a machine which actually moves the pieces on a board in obedience to these solutions). We see that this robot functions in terms of recognizing features in its environment, in accordance with the programme that has been given it. It gets its solutions according to algorithms. Now Dennett argues that artificial intelligence is real intelligence (though produced in an artificial way) if it functions as well as human intelligence, that is, if it comes up with solutions as good as or better than those a human would produce. And it is quite possible to agree with this, but still to be dubious about reductionism. For intelligence in a human, or any other animal, is not and cannot be an isolated function. We exercise our intelligence on that which we perceive and then reflect upon. But none of these perceptions or reflections are without emotional concommitants. Categories are framed, and applied, in conjunction with values. Even chess players and mathematicians, the most abstract of humans, and the least like other animals, need to be motivated by their enjoyment of problem-solving before they will give their minds to chess or mathematics. And they can be distracted from such activities by pain or acute anxiety.

And so Dennett is in difficulties when he raises the question whether a computer can feel pain. For he recognizes that while a computer could, in theory, be constructed so as to respond to stimuli in a manner exactly paralleled by the way in which humans respond to such stimuli (and he concedes that much more would need to be known about the physiology of pain before appropriate stimuli could be devised), yet the meaning of pain might still be thought to be lacking. A computer might be constructed to say 'This is awful'; but can we suppose that what was happening would actually be awful or seem awful to the computer? It will be seen that here we come back to the matter of consciousness, and with it the question of meanings. At the end of this article Dennett suggests that the reason why we find it difficult to conceive of a robot, or computer, that would feel pain may be because we have an incoherent idea of what pain actually is; and that advances in science might lead us to a better notion: 'If and when good physiological theory of pain is developed a robot could in principle be constructed to instantiate it. Such advances...would probably bring in their train wide-scale changes in what we found intuitive about pain...In the meantime, thoughtful people would refrain from kicking such a robot' (*Brainstorms*, p. 229). But I may still ask 'Why?' What would be my motive for refraining? I might believe that the robot would have been programmed to recognize that a kick required an aggressive response, and if I kicked the robot it might retaliate. I still should not refrain from kicking it on the same grounds that I refrain from kicking a person who is irritating me. Dennett himself, earlier in the same article, seems to be aware of this: 'There can be no denying...that our concept of pain is inextricably bound up with...our ethical intuitions, our sense of suffering, obligation and evil.' And he suggests that it is possible to argue that pain is, in his words, 'essentially a biological phenomenon, essentially bound up with birth, death, the reproduction of the species and even (in the case of human pain) social interractions and interrelations'. He even admits that if this sort of belief can be sustained, then 'the computer scientist trying to synthesize pain in a robot is on a fool's errand. He can no more succeed than a master cabinet maker, with the finest tools and materials, can succeed in making today a genuine Hepplewhite chair' (p. 197).

Nothing Dennett suggests seems to me to weaken the force of this objection of his own. The simple-minded answer to the question why we cannot make a computer that feels pain is that we cannot because no computer we could make would be alive. Pain is part of the value system which belongs essentially to the biological world, to animals which categorize and remember the world, and use their acquired knowledge according to their own value-systems, and this whether they are octopuses or chimpanzees or humans. All animals attach a value to pain, that is they dislike it and seek to avoid it. Their actual living brains develop each individually according to the experiences they have had of this thing, pain, which, over the millennia, they have learned to avoid.

There is one odd consequence of regarding the brain as a computer. Though such functionalism is, as I have said, reductionist, in that it seeks to explain human thought and feeling in physical terms, thus bringing together all the contents of the material world, yet in another way it serves to separate the mind from the body. The suggestion is that the body, the brain and central nervous system are the hardware, the input through the senses the software; and representations are made in the brain in accordance with the way things are in the world. The categories of things are fixed once and for all, and in accordance with these categories calculations can be made by the computer-mind, and conclusions reached. The crucial aspect of human intelligence is the ability to use the software to produce conclusions. What the hardware is like does not really matter, except that it is uniform, wherever it occurs, while the software may vary. There are fixed rules according to which the inputs are dealt with by the mind. They are extremely complex, that much is granted; and connections are made, as in any computational system, with great rapidity. But in principle there is no important difference between one system and another. The software will in practice be different. But theoretically there could be many identical computer-brains, producing identical solutions to problems, even though there will necessarily be numerous different biological bodies. This in turn suggests that the outcome of the activities of the brain, the solutions to problems, could be regarded as having an existence of their own. Rather in the way that Knowledge, regarded impersonally as What is Known, could be stored in libraries or on disc after the last human had died, so the robot's solutions to chess problems, its way of thought, could outlast any human chess players.

In contrast with a physical theory of the brain, a biological theory has the advantage of showing that each individual is unique. Not only has the species homo sapiens evolved over the centuries to reach the position it has, possessed of primary consciousness, the anatomical capacity to articulate a complex and diverse language, and the higher consciousness which goes with the use of this language, but each member of the species can be seen to develop its own awareness of the world, its own value system and its own system of categories and symbols, restricted only by the genes it has inherited. The individuality and structural diversity of brains even within one species is confounding to models that consider the brain to be a computer. Evidence derived from those studies of the development of early embryos which are now possible suggests that there is a great diversity, anatomically, in the complex ramifications of neural networks. That degree of individual diversity could not be tolerated in a computer system following instructions. But it is just what is needed in a selective system. At the embryonic stage the brain apparently organizes itself. The cells move about and interconnect with each other in unpredictable ways. That is to say that the system of the brain is statistically variable. And so, though embryos of the same species have their cells organized in broadly similar ways, there is no such thing as uniformity.

It is not to be wondered at, therefore, that each one of us thinks of himself as a unique individual; for so we all are. Not only are our bodies distinct from each other's as spatio-temporal objects, but our way of perceiving, thinking and remembering, the actual pathways through which this is achieved are not, microscopically, identical one with another. Our consciousness has developed, in detail, as our own.

Every object in the world has a history, that is it has a past which brought it to where it is in the present. In the case of human individuals, with their higher consciousness, it is possible for them to detach themselves from the present, and think of things out of time, to contemplate their own history or indeed the history of the universe. A man, alone among animals as far as we know, is able to do more than survey the present scene, illuminated by the beam of primary consciousness, but to cast light on things outside the room he has entered. He can think of how he got where he is, and even more crucially, of where he intends to go next. Moreover, being by now a language-user, he is necessarily aware of other people besides himself. Though the formation of concepts seems to lead directly to the naming of those concepts (while merely categorizing the world could stop at acting and remembering things); and though it may be that one can hardly distinguish concept-forming from language-using, yet the whole purpose of language is not merely to name thoughts, but to communicate them.

It seems to me therefore that the idea of a person who has a discernible identity through time is an idea that is, in an important sense, social. To think of myself as a continuous individual human is necessarily to acknowledge that there are other human persons in the same boat. Humans have evolved sufficiently to realize that they are members of a species of similar animals, and it is to this realization that their development of language has led them. A man, a member of the species homo sapiens, is a continuous being in the same way as a cat is a continuous being, though of different species. The complexity of human identity, the feeling we have of the importance of our own identity, arises out of the complexity of our brains compared with those of cats. We can not only be identified by someone else as persisting through time; we can so identify ourselves by the operation of conscious memory, and the consequent ability to project ourselves forward into the future, as well as backwards into the past, to tell stories about how we came to be where we are. Such, then, more or less, is the biological concept of an individual. The lesson we learn from looking at the matter in this light is that each individual is unique, his brain being uniquely developed at the embryonic stage, categorizing and recategorizing, according to unique sets of circumstances in his environment. Though his sense of identity belongs with his memory, he need not be thought to remember everything that he has done in order that we may ascribe his actions to him, for we can identify him as a single continuing member of the species without his being able consciously to remember anything at all, just as we can identify our cat as a single individual cat. If he is so totally amnesiac, we regard him as a damaged human; for most humans remember at least a fair number of the actions we ascribe to them, though by no means all. Yet even if a man remembers nothing, he is still the same man as he was, in the biological sense. In my view, this is the only way in which talking about individual men (or indeed about individual cats) makes sense. They could not live their lives normally or organize their experience without memory. But the nature of this memory is a function of their developing brain.

It follows that to identify myself is to identify my body, including its brain; and to tell the story of my life is to express my awareness of this body that has persisted through time, and look back with the aid of imagination to make sense of, or interpret, the past. In the next chapter, I shall examine some of the ways in which autobiographers have sought to establish permanent and lasting truths out of their own temporal and ephemeral experiences. There is no doubt that not just any story will perform this transformation. It cannot be done unless it is a true story of what it was like to be that individual person, who is the same person as is now alive, and who sees himself as essentially one human among many, with whom he wishes to communicate the truth of how it was.

7

Autobiography

Having considered the nature of personal identity, and concluded that the notion of human individuality is essentially biological, in this chapter I shall explore some of the reasons why man, though in Sartre's words 'a thing among things', nevertheless has immortal longings, which he sometimes hopes to satisfy by asserting his own personal continuity with the past, through the writing of autobiography. When I speak of autobiography in this connection, I mean that kind of autobiography, not especially common, which attempts to tell the truth about how things were, and what they were like, not in a spirit of boastfulness, nor in order to set the record straight about events in the public arena, but simply because the enterprise seems worth doing for itself. This kind of writing includes the autobiographical novel.

There is a sense in which autobiographical writing, if it comes off and absorbs the attention of the reader, must always seem a kind of triumph. This is because talking about our inner, private life, attempting to convey our sentiments in words which have their meaning in the outside shared world, must always be a struggle, akin to the struggle we may sometimes have to convey to ourselves the nature of a dream which haunts us, but is only half recalled. How can we express the atmosphere, or verbally depict the emotion-charged scene? If we seem to have done so, the result is valuable for its own sake, in the way that poetry is valuable.

But this is not all. In addition we value the sense of continuity which truthfully telling the story of lives gives us, not only because we value ourselves, and our ability, if we can achieve it, to communicate with others, but because, valuing our own continuity, we come to be aware of something more impervious to time than our own individual selves. We know very well that we are mortal, that each one of us will perish; and this, indeed, creates a sense of urgency that we should get something down, as we might say, so that it will not all be lost. Yet in another way we may feel that it cannot all be lost. Our sense of continuity with the past, and with the future, carries with it an obscure sense of timelessness, past, present and future amalgamated into one. Simply to be able imaginatively to embrace the past and the future from the perspective of the present has this consequence. We ourselves will not survive, and, except in the most superficial sense would not, probably, want to, but we feel ourselves to be a part of something that *has* survived and *will* survive, and which we value as we value our lives. We cannot ascribe such a sense of eternity to animals other than humans. Even if obscurely they felt that they belonged to the world as a whole, they could not tell us. We can say it about them, but they cannot say it, or think it, of themselves.

We have arrived here at the borderline between memory, with its implicit sense of continuity, and imaginative literature. The novelist Henry Green wrote his autobiography at the beginning of the Second World War. He regarded it as a substitute for a novel. Seeking to explain his writing about himself, at the beginning of *Pack My Bag* he wrote thus:

> I was born a mouth-breather with a silver spoon in 1905, three years after one war and nine before another, too late for both. But not too late for the war that seems to be coming upon us now...That is my excuse, that we who may not have time to write anything else must do the best we can. If we have no time to chew another book over, we must turn to what first comes to mind, and that must be how one changed from boy to man, how one lived, things and people and one's attitude. All these otherwise would be used in novels, material is better in that form, or any other that is not directly personal, but we feel we no longer have time. We should be taking stock. (Henry Green, *Pack My Bag*, The Hogarth Press, 1939, p. 5)

Taking stock is, of course, the sorting through of possessions before they can get lost or confused, in order to see what they are and to value them. The material, that is the truths, could have been used as the content of imaginative literature as Henry Green would have preferred (thinking, probably, with Aristotle that poetry is more philosophical than history, that is, has more universality). But, as he recognizes, the use to which he does put it is also an exercise of the imagination. For it involves the search after expression in language of what the author knows, from his own case. We may learn from writers themselves what they think they have achieved in encapsulating, or discursively setting out, the content of their memory, and transforming what might seem purely private or ephemeral into something else. And let us not forget the fact that, in so far as language is necessarily shared, that which is finally expressed linguistically must take for granted a measure of common understanding, or sympathy.

To claim to remember something is to claim to know what it was like, because I was physically and geographically there and have not forgotten. There is thus a truth-claim in my account of what I remember, a claim which, in some cases, cannot be challenged. I quote from Henry Green again:

> If I say I remember, as it seems to me I do, one of the maids, that poor thing whose breath smelled, come in one morning to tell us that the Titanic had gone down, it may be that much later they told me that I should have remembered, at the age I was then, and that their saying this had suggested that I did remember. But I do know, and they would not, that her breath was bad, that when she knelt down to do one up in front it was all one could do to stand there. (ibid., p. 9)

No one except he could have this direct knowledge. It was part of what linked him as he wrote to him then, the little boy. It is the same person who was buttoned up by the maid after the sinking of the Titanic as the person who wrote in 1939. The truth-claim is based on the continuity between then and now. Henry Green can claim to know only because he is the same person who has survived from then till now. It is, moreover, an aspect of truth that it should be timelessly true, not true just for now. We recognize that, trivial as the truth may be, if it is thus based on knowledge it is a truth that can stand for ever. For we do not, as Plato did, demand that the objects of knowledge should be grand and mysterious forms of things, outside the world.

Perhaps this needs elaboration. If I state that today is Monday, and that a steady rain is falling outside my window in Wiltshire, there is a sense in which if what I say is true, it is true on a particular day and at a particular place. It will not necessarily be true in that place tomorrow, or at another place at the time when I utter the truth. Nevertheless, in recording how something was at a particular time and place, I am saying something which is part of a history. It does not, as it were, go out of existence or lose its truth the moment it is uttered. It remains as something that can be recognized as history long after the rain has stopped and the day given place to another. It is only because the example is trivial and of no particular interest in itself that we may be tempted to deny this. No one is likely to want to contemplate the timeless truth of my statement about the rain. However, if the subject-matter were politically or socially important, if it had emotional significance for the utterer, if, like the maid with bad breath, it was a part of the truth of the childhood of someone whose childhood we were engaged in recreating, then we could seize on this truth and accept it as part of the whole scheme of things we were trying to understand. Henry Green's statement about the maid was uttered from a particular point of view (indeed, this is the basis of its unique claim to truth; no one could know it except he). Yet because it was uttered in a common language, anyone using that language could understand it. It rests on the presumption of sympathy between different humans, without which language could not function at all. Of course, such sympathy is not absolute. People may, as Wittgenstein said (*Philosophical Investigations*, p. 223) be transparent to us, or they may be a complete enigma. He says 'We learn this when we come into a strange country with entirely strange traditions; and, what is more, even given a mastery of the country's language.' And he says 'If a lion could talk, we could not understand him.' Yet we rely on a sympathy with other humans. And the personal and momentary may be transformed into the potentially universal and timeless on the basis of that sympathy. We and our successors may equally read *Pack My Bag* and enter into the world of Henry Green. And so his world persists, simply because he described it. Being a writer by profession, he intended that this should be so. It was what he wrote for. But the same effect can be achieved sometimes by accident, if, for example, an old letter falls into your hands, and the person who wrote it and her world are suddenly brought vividly before you. At the centre of this transformation (itself the centre of the creation of a work of art) lies the self, the unique individual who lives or has lived his own life, and sees things from behind his own eyes. If lions, as opposed to humans, have such selves, we cannot know them, and therefore cannot value them as we value humans. Through autobiography, the world of the individual becomes general or universal because it becomes part of history, in the understanding of which, as I hope to have suggested (see chapter 5), we exercise our imagination to grasp what ceases to belong to any particular time. In writing, or in reading autobiography, we strive to make time immaterial, as it is to all universal truths.

Now the growth of autobiographical writing coincided with the Romantic concentration on the self, and the belief that all knowledge was, in some sense, self knowledge. As I have already argued, Kant's *Critique of Pure Reason* provided a philosophical justification for making the self thus central. For according to Kant we construct an intelligible world out of undifferentiated messages which come to us through the senses according to *a priori* categories (instantiated, he thought, in logic). It is the understanding which grasps the laws; it is the intuition and imagination which supply the universe to be thus rendered orderly and intelligible. But none of this construction could be done if the rational perceiving creature did not provide a unity, a point of view from which the world was to be perceived by him. So the 'I' is at the centre of the world, yet applies laws to the content of its own perception which are universally necessary. In the light of these laws, the world becomes a common, shared world intelligible in the same terms to everyone. Kant's theory of intelligibility was not, of course, supposed to be empirical. Evidence was thus irrelevant to it. Nevertheless, as I have suggested, it is not absurd to see in it a theoretical foreshadowing of the kind of empirical theory of brain-function outlined in the last chapter. It is the developing categorizing function of the brain that, in humans, develops so highly that it gives rise to self-awareness and to language, in terms of which the universe of each individual is recognized as a shared and universally intelligible universe, intelligible, that is, to all members of the same species.

Kant distinguished the *a priori* self, the 'vehicle of all concepts' about which nothing could be said, from the empirical self, who in the already perceived and ordered world had a particular history, and had acquired a particular set of concepts. Those Romantics, such as Wordsworth who had not read Kant, and those like Coleridge who had done so, after a fashion, abandoned this distinction. And so truths about oneself could transform into truths about the world at large, the individual becoming the medium through which the whole common intelligible world must be explored. Wordsworth believed that his own specific childhood, the traces left on him by his boyhood in the Lake District, not only affected his own subsequent life, but gave access to quite general truths which he could render intelligible to all who read his autobiographical poems, and which he had a positive duty to enunciate. *The Prelude* can be read as an attempt to show how Wordsworth's particular memory images came to be transformed into universal ideas, and thus to be valued in a wholly new way. The forms impressed on him by Nature, to use his own terminology, determined not only his aesthetic but his moral sensibilities, giving rise to concepts of man's place in the universe that were universal in their significance. It was not simply that natural beauty caused him to think of eternal or moral values. It was that the forms themselves, the powerful images, imprinted on him as they were, *meant* these value-truths. They were themselves significant of these values. There could be no other access to the truths he felt himself bound to enunciate than through the contemplation of his own particular and unique past, which was continuous with the present, and the images of which still existed in his brain and in his blood.

The existence of such persistent images, recollections which can in principle be described, is precisely what makes us inclined to say that memory is a species of imagination. For the images or thoughts which constitute these memories are thoughts of something not present to us now. Moreover, like other products of the imagination, the images recalled frequently have a significance unrelated to a specific event. Thus, the memories associated with childhood may or may not have relation to particular events. Often they do not. If you give me the command 'think of the dog you had as a child', then if I had a dog, I may summon up an image, or otherwise recall some features of that specific animal's character, without reference to any occasions when I was with him, which may have been too numerous to recall one by one. I produce a generalized memory. But now suppose that I never had a dog. You might command me to imagine one, an animal of the kind that perhaps I would like to have owned. If I produce an image of a kind of dog, my way of thinking would, it seems to me, be the same in either case. It is only that, in the former case and not the latter, my imaginative thought is concerned with a particular animal who once existed. Whether or not there ever was such an animal is not a matter of my way of thinking of it, but rather of history. Do the archives reveal that I ever had a dog? Are there contemporary photographs, or confirming recollections from my siblings? These are external criteria for deciding whether my thought is a memory or not. There are no internal criteria. And so as I have argued, conscious memory, or recollection, must be regarded as a sub-species of imagination.

Those philosophers, including Locke, Hume, Russell and many others, who discussed the nature of memory had, all of them, great difficulty in deciding how an idea might be recognized as an idea of memory rather than one of imagination. That is to say, they would have agreed, in a sense, with my argument that an imaginative thought or image and one of memory were qualitatively alike, in so far as the one could be easily taken for the other. But they argued that there must be some way of telling an idea of memory from one of imagination, intrinsic to the idea itself. This insistence was part of the more general belief that the mind is a separate entity from the body, and that therefore the contents of the mind must somehow be capable of being described from within, without reference to the body, or to anything that lies 'outside the mind'. They were therefore faced with the question what it was about certain of our ideas which referred them to the past. Various devices were attempted to identify this 'pastness'. Hume thought that plainly the ideas of memory had much greater vivacity, were simply livelier, than ideas of imagination. Hobbes suggested the precise opposite, that memory ideas were peculiarly weak compared with the others; William James held that the ideas of memory possessed a certain 'warmth and intimacy' lacking to ideas of imagination; Russell said that they were accompanied by a feeling of familiarity and of pastness. I shall not pursue these attempts to characterize memory; since I have argued that memory is a kind of imagination, and since there is no good reason to think that there need be a safe way of telling from within that an idea is one of memory rather than some other kind of imagination, we can content ourselves with saying that for an idea or thought to be properly referred to as a memory, it must have been caused by a past experience of that person whose memory it is claimed to be. We often believe that what we claim to remember is so certain that it cannot be doubted. Thomas Reid put it thus:'A belief which we have from distinct memory we account real knowledge, no less certain than if it were grounded on demonstration; no man in his wits calls it in question' (Thomas Reid, *Essay on the Intellectual Powers of Man*, 1785). Henry Green, who is much puzzled in his autobiography by the question how one can know something is a real memory, not derived from later hearsay, concludes that on the whole 'memories of early days seem true' (*Pack My Bag*, p. 55). In any case, memory-claims are claims to knowledge, and, like other such claims, they are not self-guaranteeing, even if, often, we are inclined to accept them. When we do accept them, it is not only because they 'seem true' but because they have an intrinsic plausibility, given other things we know. I might tell my children, and sincerely believe myself, that I saw a German band marching down the road where I lived as a child. For a long time I believed that I remembered it. I could see myself, holding my mother's hand at the gate, and the grey-khaki of the uniforms and the characteristic helmets, and the sound of the brass. Only later did I realize that this could not be a true memory, but very probably a dream remembered, or a remembered image derived from something I was told; for there were no German bands in this country after the First World War, when I was not alive.

Another complicating factor here is that we may, and frequently do, misremember. That is, I may claim to remember something, and, though it was true that I was there when the event occurred, I have remembered it wrong. My mistake in such a case, too, could be shown from external evidence. I do not believe that the fact that we may remember wrong, or just vaguely and imprecisely, is of great theoretical importance. For, on the other hand, some of our memory claims are not only justified, but are some of the very strongest claims to knowledge that we can ever make. Among such strong claims are those we make when we recall what something was like, how it struck us, what the atmosphere was. These are recollections which are generally the most highly charged emotionally; and often it is a source of enormous pleasure, or pain, to relive such emotions. Their truth is vouched for by their effect on us. The central element of all such claims to knowledge is the continuity that exists between me then and me now. Not only could a history be traced by someone else, or by documentary evidence, of how it came about that I, the same physical object, the same human being, was there then and am here now, but also, in the strongest cases, there is a felt continuity, an emotional continuity, between my past and my present. Such was the case with Henry Green's recollection of his nursemaid.

This element, whether experienced emotionally or not, is the continuity of a 'thing among things'. Just as I or anyone else can refer to the same table or the same cat or the same stone as was here last year, so I, or someone else, can refer to the same person who had those experiences then, and is here now to tell the tale. My memory has at least a good chance of being true if my body, including my brain, is the same thing as it was all those years ago, subject, of course, to the sorts of gradual change over the years that humans and other living organisms undergo. We do not need an internal or purely mental criterion to determine whether a thought is a memory thought. It can be taken to be such, if I say that it is, and if there could in principle be shown that there was then a physical object, me, continuous with the physical object that is me now. That we may sometimes fall into error about our memories does not invalidate all our claims to know, when knowledge is derived from this source.

In memory, then, we have a kind of imagination that bears a special relation with truth, and hence with understanding. The designation of it as imagination is not unjustified. Not only is recollection a way, as I have argued, of thinking of something in its absence, as all imaginative thinking is, but it can form the basis of creativity at the highest level. Recollection reflected on, as Wordsworth maintained, can contain a significance which goes far beyond the individual whose recollection it is. Its significance demands to be expressed, and the purpose of its expression is to reveal a truth, and make it available to whoever cares to hear it.

Wordsworth's *Prelude* is a monument to the claims of creative recollection, new, as I suggested above, to the Romantic age. It is not only an autobiography, but an exploration of the nature of that recollection which goes into creating the story of a life. Recollection itself is both the deliberately recurring theme, and is shown to be the point or meaning of the telling of the story. The story explores the significance of a remembered past. In this respect it is a precursor of Proust's autobiographical novel, *Remembrance of Things Past*. Nowhere is the significance of a remembered past more insisted on, analysed and indeed exploited for aesthetic purposes than in this novel. Earlier, in chapter 2, I noticed the meaning of the word 'joy', used by Coleridge to designate the imaginative power essential to a poet. 'Joy' was the strength of feeling in the contemplation of a significant or symbolic object, which could be communicated through a poem or other work of art. It was essentially creative, and was intrinsically valuable. It was the loss of this joy that Coleridge lamented in what is in fact one of his great masterpieces, the *Ode: Dejection*. Proust uses the same word, 'la joie', for the essence of creative genius; and, for him, this joy was related necessarily to recollection, and the knowledge which arises directly from recollection and from no other source. There is an extraordinary parallel between the loss of joy recorded in Coleridge's Ode (where he said of himself that he could 'see, not feel' how beautiful things were) and the similar sterility recorded by Proust, just before the great revelation came to him of what he must do with the past, how he must use it.

He describes how he, the narrator, had come out of a sana-
torium, his health not improved and his depression acute. Sitting
in the train, he looks out of the window and carefully observes
the appearance of the trees outside: ' "Trees", I thought, "you
have nothing more to tell me, my cold heart hears you no
more. I am in the midst of Nature, yet it is with boredom
that my eyes observe the line which separates your luminous
countenance from your shaded trunks. If ever I believed myself
a poet, I now know that I am not one" ' (Proust, *Remembrance
of Things Past*, trans. Stephen Hudson, Chatto and Windus,
1944, vol. 12, *Time Regained*, p. 195). The next day, convinced that he would never again experience any but superficial
feelings, in the total absence of creative power, he reflected
on his condition, and tried deliberately to conjure up some
memories of Venice, where he had felt intensely, in the past.
He succeeded in calling up images of Venice, mental 'snapshots';
but they had no significance. The very word 'Venice' filled him
with boredom, and his mental 'snapshots' did no more for him
than an exhibition of someone else's photographs. Suddenly,
however, as he left his carriage for a party, everything changed.
In the courtyard he stumbled, and, in recovering, he stepped
on an uneven paving-stone. At the sensation of the uneven
paving-stone, he was immediately flooded by a sense of amazing
delight, a vision which seemed to float over him, commanding
him to grasp it, if he could, and solve the riddle of the happiness it offered. And then he recognized Venice in what he felt,
the very Venice which his conscious effort had failed to recreate.
For he had stepped on an uneven paving-stone before, in the
Baptistry of St Mark, and his present sensation had given
Venice back to him, with all the other sensations belonging to
that past. When he went into the house, plainly in a state of
heightened awareness, two more experiences followed, the sound
of a servant knocking a spoon against a plate, and the sensation
of pressing his lips against a starched napkin, each of which
immediately transported him back to a different time in his past
life. He was suddenly aware of the complete difference that
exists between the artificial meaning we try to give the past
when we deliberately attempt to recall it, whether by images or
intellectual reconstructions, and the significance it has when we
relive the past through spontaneous memory. Then and only

then, according to Proust, the meaning of the past comes with
our recollection, and shows us the truth. This truth is not truth
that could be discovered by revisiting the places where we had
been before, and which are now recalled. The narrator, he tells
us, had tried that, and had always been disappointed. For the
truth lies not in the place but in ourselves. The imagination has
as its only function to grasp what is absent. And so going back
to a place and rendering it present will not in itself help the
imagination. Rather the contrary. When the imagination deliberately tries to recreate what is absent, whatever the means
employed, the absent object has no foothold in reality. According to Proust, it is only when a past sensation is spontaneously
called to mind by a present sensation, the stones of Venice by
the stones in the courtyard of the Guermantes' Palace, where
both are experienced together, that a contact is made between
the dreams of imagination, and 'that of which they are habi-
tually deprived, namely the idea of existence'. The existence of
the past, that is to say, is assured by its encapsulation in a
present experience. Proust's narrator then determines to capture
this reality, to cause it to live longer than the moment in which
the two sensations, present and past, coexist, one overlaid on
the top of the other before evaporating. 'The only way', he says,
'was to attempt to know them more completely where they
existed, that is within myself, and by so doing to illuminate their
depths.' And there was no other means of exploration open to
him than through the creation of a work of art. The aim of such
a work, the only possible genuine work of art, as he thinks,
must be to express the knowledge that comes from such flashes
of spontaneous memory, where the authenticity of the memory,
the truth that it contains, is self-guaranteeing; it is known
immediately, and could not be doubted. According to Proust,
it is possible to reconstruct the past in this truthful way, because

> if we see again a thing which we looked at formerly, it brings
> back to us, together with our past vision, all the imagery with
> which it was instinct. This is because objects, as soon as they
> have been perceived by us, become something immaterial within
> us, partake of the same nature as our preoccupations or our
> feelings at that time, and combine indissolubly with them. (ibid.,
> p. 233)

And so it is that in writing the truth, a writer must search
within himself, and seek to extract the significance of what
happened in the past and link it with the present. Mere description, on this theory, though it may claim to be realistic, cannot
be properly called true. Truth consists in what is meant by an
impression or a spoken word. 'In describing objects', Proust
says, 'one can make those things which figure in a particular
place succeed one another indefinitely; the truth will begin to
emerge only from the moment that the writer takes two different objects, posits their relationship and encloses it within
the circle of "style"'. I understand this to mean that a writer,
if he is to illuminate by his imaginative telling of the autobiographical story, has to relate the past with the present,
through his own continuity. His 'style', or personality, is what
he is now. It is only this continuity of sensibility that can break
through the superficial appearances of things and give them a
significance which, if he is successful as an imaginative writer,
if, that is, he has imaginative genius, will be a permanent or
timeless significance. Proust ends this long discussion thus: 'To
write that essential book, which is the only true one, a writer
does not in the ordinary sense of the word invent it, but since
it exists already in each one of us, he interprets it. The duty
and the task of a writer are those of an interpreter.'

The specific interpretative faculty of Proust's theory was
recollection. So the 'only book', the necessary true book that
he had to write, was in the form of a story, a coherent story of
himself as a creature with a history. For the truth he was trying
to express was said to lie within himself, and had therefore to
be told from behind his own eyes. It had to be autobiographical,
even if disguised autobiography. True autobiography is not
simply a matter, if there could be such a matter, of writing
down what happened, one event after another, in the life of
the author. It must have some point, that is, it must involve a
particular interpretation of what happened. Wordsworth need
not have written his autobiographical poem the way he did. He
wrote it thus in order to illuminate what he held to be a quite
general truth, namely that recollection colours our whole life,
gives it value and renders it intelligible, and that therefore it
can and should be shared. He felt an obligation to express as
intelligibly, and therefore as intensely, as he could his 'spots of

time' (his moments of intense awareness, which therefore had intense significance), both what they were like at the time and the moral insight that he now thought they engendered; and his life made sense to him when regarded in this light.

At a less elevated level it is certainly true that we sometimes attempt to make sense of something that has happened to us by, as it were, re-running it in our imagination, and trying to interpret it as we do so (and this is yet further proof that memory and imagination cannot be distinguished in practice). Consider this case: a girl says goodbye to her lover at the station. She is confident that they will, as they generally do, meet again very soon. He says 'What are you thinking?' She says 'I'm thinking that I'm very happy'. He says 'I'm glad'. Now days and weeks have passed, and she has not heard from him. She goes over and over the conversation at the station, hearing in her mind's ear exactly the tones in which he and she spoke, reliving the scene in her imagination; and she comes to the conclusion that he meant to convey that he was breaking with her. He didn't want to say so, and have to witness her distress, or listen to possible reproaches. He genuinely wanted them to part happily, as indeed they did. After all, she reasons, why didn't he say he would write, or urge her to write? Why didn't he say anything about ringing up? He must have decided in advance to leave her, and was doing it in a civilized, not unfriendly way. She frequently thinks about ringing him up or writing, but, so convinced is she of her interpretation of what happened, that she argues that she must not pester him, if that is what he wants. Pride will not permit her to try to get in touch. She knows that there could be other interpretations of what happened. He could have fallen ill. He might have tried and failed to ring her and have decided that she wanted to avoid him. But these alternatives do not persuade. They seem to have no authenticity. She now knows, or believes that she knows, the story as it was, and must try to see her life in future in the light of this past as she has written it for herself. We can of course continue the story in any way we like, into an imagined future. We can conceive of future meetings when all will be revealed; we can suppose that he was murdered on his way back from the station. But for her now, with the future still uncertain, she has chosen the story she believes, and feels she must believe to be true; and she has chosen it on the basis of her re-running of her mental tape of the conversation.

Such is the general case with autobiography. Autobiographers construct a story of their past life, partly, it is true, out of records, family histories, their own or other people's contemporary diaries and letters, but partly and most importantly from re-running in their imagination what their memory tells them things were like, and what those things meant for them at the time, and mean for them now, in their different, but nevertheless identical, selves, as they sit down to write. It is, obviously, crucial to autobiography that the person who writes is the same person as that whose story is told. This is indeed a blindingly obvious point; but it is important in this way. A story has a hero, a central character. The story makes sense as it evolves around that character who gives it its meaning. We can and do give sense to our own lives by constructing them as a story. And to give sense to something is to give sense not just for ourselves, but for others.

So it is finally worth looking again at what people say when they attempt to explain their motives in writing about themselves in the past; for nearly everyone who writes autobiography feels it necessary to explain why they are undertaking what might seem a pure exercise in self-aggrandizement, a signal of galloping self-absorption, as we saw in the case of Henry Green.

Richard Coe in his book about this form of art (*Autobiography and the Experience of Childhood*, Yale University Press, 1985) says this: 'If the isolated self is to be transmuted into something durably significant, [the volume] needs to possess a vitality and originality which is very far from common; and it needs further to be spurred on by the imperious urge to impart a message or to impart a truth which may not be allowed to vanish'. The imperious urge to impart a message was certainly what motivated Wordsworth, and also Proust. For Proust, his book was the 'necessary' and the 'only true' book. For Wordsworth there was an absolute duty to explain the moral significance and recreative power of memory and imagination itself:

...what we have loved
Others will love; and we will teach them how;
Instruct them how the mind of man becomes
A thousand times more beautiful than the earth
On which he dwells
(*Prelude* Bk XIV, 11426–450)

Some authors, less than plausibly, in my view, argue that human affairs repeat themselves, and that therefore to be told of the decisions and reactions of one person, as honestly as they can be told, will help other people when faced with the same situation in future years. Thus Stephen Spender, in the introduction to his autobiography, says 'I believe obstinately that if I am able to write with truth about what happened to me, this can help others who have to live through the same sort of thing' (*World within World*, Faber, 1950, re-issued 1985). He therefore holds it unnecessary for autobiographers to bother their readers with any account of their backgrounds, origins, or even their childhood, but should plunge straight into the account of their adult experiences. It should be noticed that he does not quite follow this advice; and that the best parts of his book are those about his childhood and adolescence. Moreover, if this view of autobiography were followed too relentlessly, the role of memory and the imaginative interpretation of memory would tend to drop away. A collection of moralistic fables could perform the same warning and instructive function.

Other writers, however, in my view much more plausibly, avoid both the idea of explicit moralizing, and that of recurrences in history, and concentrate instead on the notion of truth itself. Thus, for example, the Australian writer Hal Porter, at the beginning of the story of his childhood, writes 'Of this house, of what takes place within it until I am six, I alone can tell. That is perhaps why I must tell. No one but I will know if a lie be told, therefore I must try for the truth' (*The Watcher on the Cast-iron Balcony*, Faber, 1963, p. 6). That there is no criterion of truth except his own certainty, when he gets the expression of it right, makes this high duty of truthfulness all the more demanding. The writer speaks of himself, and he himself is his only and inescapable judge.

It is of the greatest importance, it seems to me, that the point of writing autobiography, or indeed any kind of history, should be seen to be to 'try for the truth'. We must not lose grip on this, to my mind, obvious fact. And we may feel confident that if we get to the truth, or even near it, this will be recognized by our readers. It is that and only that which can make the story worth reading. The last autobiographer I shall quote makes this point clearly and explicitly. Storm Jamieson in her autobiography writes in the preface:

> The man or woman who has lived an uncommon life, or who has played a part in some great undertaking...need not offer any further reason why he or she wants to record it. Some other reason or excuse is needed when the life brought out to be judged is nothing out of the way. My first and less egotistical excuse is that my memory, an exceptionally good one, contains three ages, the one that ended in August 1914, the one between November 1918 and August 1945, and the present, which may not have much of a future. The second and stronger reason, no more and no less egotistical than the impulse to write a novel is the wish to discover before it is too late what sort of person I have been, without allowing vanity or cleverness to soften the outline of the creature. I am an accomplished professional novelist, and nothing would have been easier for me than to draw a portrait which, without telling a single lie, would be dishonest from beginning to end, charming, interesting and a lie. I have tried to write with perfect sincerity, without malice towards others or myself. A degree of failure was implicit in the effort from the start, and a degree of distortion, however many precautions I took not to lie. But if I had not thought the effort worthwhile to others besides myself I should not have made it. It is improbable that the glass I have been looking into for the last four or five years reflects only my own mind and heart. (Jamieson, *Journey from the North*, Collins, 1969, p. xii)

The fact is that human beings delight in communication, and the urge to communicate to others what it was like. To explain oneself, not in the sense of an apologetic, but simply on the assumption that other people will understand if one tells the truth, is a very powerful urge. The belief in human sympathy is not only the underlying belief which alone makes the attempt to tell the truth intelligible; it also represents the basis of the values which we feel in our bones. It is worth trying to get things right, and to get other people to understand, not in order to make life easier for them, as Spender seemed to think, not indeed for any consequence at all, but simply because this sort of understanding is of irreducible and intrinsic value. For an autobiography, or autobiographical novel, to work, it is not necessary that its author should have led an 'important' or an 'interesting' life, judged by standards imported from politics or social history, or any of the sciences. What it needs is the search for truth, through memory and the interpreting imagination. For an individual truthfully explored, as Storm Jamieson recognized, is more than just an individual. Because human beings are bound together by sympathy, the reflection in the glass is necessarily not of one person only. The common, the shared and the general is to be found in the particular, if that particular is truthfully described, and with imagination. To discover such a common truth is an intrinsic good.

8

The Future

I turn now to that aspect of the human imagination which is concerned with our thoughts not about the past but about the future. I have already suggested that the imagination, especially as it concentrates on the past in the writing of autobiography or history, may turn a particular truth into one that is universal, or at least universally intelligible. The warranty of such truth is twofold. It lies in the fact of sympathy with humans other than ourselves, and in continuity, either the continuity between me now and me then at the time I write about, or the continuity between life now and life then, at the time about which the historian writes. These two factors, sympathy and continuity, are not disconnected. In so far as both allow us to universalize imaginatively, beyond the immediate, personal and present, they allow us also to deal with what is permanent rather than fleeting.

If we are concerned, then, with the contrast between the ephemeral and the permanent (as we inevitably are in both autobiography and history), we cannot fail to think of religion as a source of imaginative inspiration, perhaps even of authority, in this field. I believe that those philosophers (the majority in the twentieth century, at least) who hold that religion is totally irrelevant to philosophy are mistaken. (I am not of course forgetting that there are philosophers who interest themselves in the Philosophy of Religion; but this is a different matter.) I do not think that philosophy can be practised in a totally non-historical context; and if we look at the history of Western Philosophy, how it came to be where it is now, the influence of religion is manifest. One of the best and most relevant examples of this influence is the effect of the Church on

Descartes. It is sometimes argued that Descartes wrote the *Discourse on Method* and the *Meditations* specifically in order to show that God was at the centre of his thinking, His existence and benevolence ultimately responsible for human knowledge. Only so could Descartes safely go on to publish his more analytic and scientific works. It is certainly plausible to suggest that he might have been sufficiently alarmed by the attitude of the Church to science to wish to put himself right with the authorities before publishing anything more empirically or scientifically adventurous. But, this apart, there is no doubt that the great Cartesian distinction between material and mental substance was, one way or another, the outcome of the Christian distinction between Soul and Body. And we cannot simply neglect the taken-for-granted background of Christian dogma as an influence on philosophy until well into the nineteenth century. As an introduction, then, to examining the relation between the imagination and the future, I shall look briefly at the idea of personal immortality, one of the central religious ideas, at least until that time, and one in which the imagination was required to stretch forward to eternity.

It is, self-evidently, the search for permanence that lies at the heart of the essentially religious idea of immortality. I have, I hope, said enough about personal identity (see chapter 6) to make it clear that, in my view, the notion of an individual human living for ever, or embarking on a new life after his death, is unsustainable. For a human is a biological entity like other animals, with a limited life-span. What he has, uniquely, is a brain sufficiently developed to enable him to think in universal terms, and to envisage things beyond the present moment. This includes his ability to think not only of his own past and future, but of the past and future in general, and of time itself, and therefore of eternity.

Eternity, or the longlasting as opposed to the ephemeral, is not a concept concerned wholly with the future. Indeed, the arguments which Plato ascribed to Socrates to prove the immortality of the soul concentrated more on the past life of the soul than on its future life, its previously acquired knowledge alone making it capable of knowledge in its life on earth. And certainly the sense of eternity (or universality and timelessness) is often engendered specifically by a sympathy with those who have inhabited the past. There have been innumerable expressions of such a sense of continuity and kinship with the past. I shall quote just two of them. The first is from an autobiography by René Cutforth. He describes how, while he was at his preparatory school, at which, up to this time, he had been intensely bored, he was sent on a run. While he stopped to rest, he found an ammonite by the gate on which he was leaning. He did not know what it was, but thought it beautiful. After a little while, as he was looking at it, one of the school masters came up, and instead of rebuking him or sending him on, stopped for conversation.

'Oh sir', I said 'what's this?' 'That's an ammonite' said Mr. Johnson, 'a fossil shell, very old, used to live here when all this land was under the sea, a long time ago.' 'Before the Romans and Ancient Britons?', I asked. 'Oh long before. About sixty million years before there were any men at all.' 'Sixty million years old? Before or after the world was made in six days?' 'Well, metaphorically,' Mr. Johnson said, 'about the Thursday of that week. Interesting period, geologically: the giant lizards, the dinosaurs, the first flying beasts, the pterodactyls...they're all still here under the ground. This part of England is full of them.' I don't know why this revelation of the huge continuity of the past should have been such a release to my imagination, but it was. It was a genuine illumination, something to do with perspective, something to do with the mysterious quality of time itself; something to do with buried treasure, something which joined the separate worlds of poetry and finding out and learning, and the splendid look of the country. (Cutforth, *Order to View*, Faber and Faber, 1969, p. 40)

Secondly, I shall quote the famous passage from Edward Gibbon:

My temper is not very susceptible of enthusiasm, and the enthusiasm I do not feel, I have ever scorned to affect. But at the distance of twenty-five years I can neither forget nor express the strong emotions which agitated my mind as I first approached and entered the Eternal City. After a sleepless night I trod, with lofty step, the ruins of the Forum; each memorable spot where Romulus stood, or Tully spoke, or Caesar fell, was

at once present to my eye; and the several days of intoxication
were lost or enjoyed before I could descend to cool and minute
investigation. (E. Gibbon, *Autobiography*, J. M. Dent, 1932,
p. 122)

And he wrote 'It was at Rome, on the 15th of October 1764,
as I sat musing among the ruins of the Capitol, while the
barefooted friars were singing Vespers in the temple of Jupiter,
that the idea of writing the decline and fall of the city first
started to my mind.' The image of the 'barefooted friars singing
Vespers in the temple of Jupiter' contains within it the whole
imaginative force of the concept of continuity.

Whether or not such imaginative revelations of eternity are
to be classified as religious must I think depend on whether
they would be so classified by those who experienced them.
I doubt whether either of the authors I have quoted would
connect them with religion. But such intimations of continuity,
the permanence of nature and life on earth, may of course
frequently be experienced in a specifically religious context.
Ancient ecclesiastical buildings, old orders of worship, music
written for use in services and so used for centuries, may evoke
a sense of permanence and a living continuity with the past
which is, at any rate, the life of Christianity. Such consciousness
of continuity is, as I have said, not separable from that human
sympathy, the understanding of how other humans think and
thought, which can make us understand that humans are all
in the same boat, a boat that has been afloat for centuries.

In so far as it is specifically Christian, the idea of continuity
is expressed partly in terms of the continuous existence of the
Church, a continuity which exists despite many schisms and
rebellions, including the Reformation itself. It was enabled so to
survive largely because of its dependence on a yet older Jewish
tradition, the idea of the Everlasting to be found in the Old
Testament, upon which the churches were founded almost as
much as they were upon the New. The idea of eternity, in this
tradition, pertained to all of God's creation. God and his handiwork will last from everlasting to everlasting, whatever particular changes there may be. Such were the ideas expressed, for
example, most frequently in the psalms upon which the ordinary
services of the Christian Church were centred, and which were

set to music and used as part of worship, wherever Christianity existed. It was here, perhaps, that the imaginative elements of Christianity most clearly expressed themselves.

It is to be noted, in passing, that whenever the Church has made efforts to exclude the aesthetic from its rituals, to separate the pleasurable from the elevating, or morally instructive, it has always failed, to a greater or lesser degree. The Church has always had an ambivalent attitude towards imagination, setting it in contrast to that understanding or revelation supposed to be the only source of truth. Moreover, the pleasures of the imagination, derived characteristically from poetry, painting and music, however deep such pleasures may be, have always seemed nonetheless to be pleasures and therefore to be foregone, if they have stood in the way of salvation, by pure faith or pure works. A more practical non-aesthetic response to the gospels has been demanded, not merely an imaginative grasp of the story, that being, after all, a response appropriate as much to fiction as to fact. Instead, what has often been required was a positive conversion, a demonstration that one cannot read and understand these stories without its changing one's life (rather as Sartre reported that, though he had read Marx as an undergraduate, he had not really understood Marx; for one could not be said to understand him unless one understood that this entailed action. There could be no such thing, he held, as an armchair Marxist. See Sartre, *The Problem of Method*, trans. Hazel Barnes, Methuen, 1963, pp. 3–31. Just so, it has been argued, there cannot be an armchair Christian). There have thus been frequent attempts to go back to the gospels, without symbolism, without extravagant rituals or ceremonies, without elaborate music. The result of these efforts in the past has generally been to change but not to destroy the central role that the aesthetic imagination must play in the acceptance of Christian dogma. We have only to think of the translation of the Latin services into the vernacular to see how the poetic genius of the English at that time, the national ear for linguistic rhythms peculiarly strong in the seventeenth century, was called in aid to produce a liturgy now frequently castigated for being too poetic, though this was not the intention. Again, the Council of Trent laid down clear guidelines for the setting of sacred texts to music specifying one note to each syllable, with no ornamentation or other purely musical embellishments. The outcome was not austerity or poverty of imagination, but an outburst of the most superb church music ever composed, including, for example, the great verse anthems of Orlando Gibbons. What came about was a new interpretation of the texts, a new understanding of them precisely through the music to which they were set. The challenge laid down by the Council of Trent was to think of the texts afresh. It was as if there were new music waiting to be written in response to this injunction. The outcome was music of such genius that it is impossible to listen to it without thinking through it to the meaning of the words. Such, in a way, had been the intention of those who dictated the change. But they could have had no idea of the miraculous creativity of those who set themselves to obey the instructions. Such happy miscalculation was possible for two reasons. First, language is inherently ambiguous, and songs especially lend themselves naturally to suggesting far more than the words alone, literally interpreted, could convey. Second, religious thought poses peculiar difficulties, when it comes to stating plainly what is meant. For religious ideas must always be expressed through metaphor and symbol. This is just the kind of meaning which music is, and was, especially fitted to convey and to enhance. As with music, so with other symbolic appurtenances of the Church. If they were taken away, nothing would be left. For religion is incapable of being literal.

The most effective symbolism is what I have called 'natural', or is at least so long-established that we can feel its meaning without instruction. It is hard to say whether the apparent 'naturalism' of musical meanings is really natural or simply long-established in culture. But I am inclined on the whole to the 'naturalist' view, since rhythmically all humans share much the same experience at a basic level. Their hearts all beat, and, being two-legged and upright, they all walk in much the same 'common time'. Moreover, it is difficult to see how certain slow rhythms and minor keys could convey anything but sorrow or solemnity. A brisk dancing dirge in six-eight time seems like a contradiction. Where someone has used an unexpected form for an apparently inappropriate mood, this has generally to be understood as ironic, the paradoxes perhaps enhancing what is conveyed, but only against the established background. In any case, whatever is the truth about musical 'meanings', it seems that if music is used successfully in religion, it must be within the context of agreed, traditional meanings, its own or those it finds in the religious texts, or, more plausibly, both together. And a religious tradition does not demand a single, literal interpretation of the doctrines handed down.

Indeed, the great enemies of the imagination, in whatever field it is exercised are, on the one hand literalness, that is, a narrow and limited idea of the truth, and on the other hand a failure of historical sense – what the historian Keith Thomas, following Lord Acton, called 'present-mindedness'. As the theologian Jaroslav Pelekan wrote 'A tradition is vindicated for each of us as an individual and for us as a community by how it manages to accord with our deepest intuitions' (Pelekan, *The Vindication of Tradition*, Yale University Press, 1984, p. 54). Now these intuitions will be concerned with our shared values, what we take seriously, what we aspire to or want to avoid. They will be concerned with what we think our place is in the universe as a whole, with our birth and death, and our feelings about the permanence, even the eternity, of the natural world. Our values are themselves largely formed by tradition, and we cannot well understand them, let alone articulate them, by attempting to stand wholly outside tradition. So how does this tradition constrain or inform us in our thoughts about the future? If there are some ways of interpreting the world that have a permanent and lasting validity, and if there are some values that we wish to assert as universally shared, then we must be able to say something about the way these will continue to exist, as well as the way they have arisen from the past.

I have argued that imagination enables us to move from the present both backwards and forwards in time. If, by means of imagination, we can think of ourselves as part of the continuity of history, and as members individually both of a community of humans, and as parts of nature as a whole, then this entails that we must so think of ourselves with regard to the future as well as to the past. For we know that this community and this nature will survive when we have died. I want now to explore some ways in which, without giving up our common sense and scientific certainty that we shall all die, we can nevertheless think of ourselves as connected with and belonging to an indefinite future. I want to suggest how we may think of ourselves as part of a life which will stretch out for our children and our children's children, and for people with whom we are in no way genetically related, a part, in short, of the Life of the World to Come. There are those who know before they die that what they have done or thought will have changed the world for ever. Their monument will be around for all to see. But such people are few, and the idea of immortality, the notion that death will be overcome, or will in some sense not be the end, is not confined to men of genius, nor even to those who would aspire to that position.

Immortality, in Christian thought, came, by devious routes, to mean that this life was a preparation for another life hereafter; and that what you did now, while you were alive in the ordinary sense of the word, had an all-important effect on your life after death. It made the difference between everlasting happiness and everlasting torment. For you personally, body and soul, would live a second time, this time for ever. Although it still gives rise to a storm of abuse if one says so, yet I cannot but think that few people could be found who seriously or literally believe this now. Nevertheless, something remains; and that is the central notion that what you do now makes a difference, not just to yourself and your immediate neighbours, but for ever, and for everyone, as long as the world exists.

Of course, compared with the notion that you must behave well in order to secure a life of bliss for yourself, or at least in order to avoid everlasting damnation (though this was always the crudest possible version of the Christian ideal), the requirement that you ought to think about what you do now for the sake of future people, who may or may not ever exist, and who will certainly be unknown to you even if they do, may seem to require a considerable degree of self-effacement – altruism, in fact. I want to pursue this idea a bit further. It is essentially connected with the fact that, for humans, there are values that endure, and are indifferent to time.

In his ingenious book *Reasons and Persons* (OUP, 1984) Derek Parfit argues that in order to bring about such self-effacement, the sense of such long-term obligation, we need radically to change the ideas we have about our own identity.

It is certainly true that in order to make sense of the notion that we may have obligations to people who will possibly never exist, and that these obligations may go on into an unending future, we need to rethink the presuppositions of, for example, utilitarianism. For the Principle of Utility, held by Bentham and J. S. Mill to be the basis of all possible morality, depends on our ability to distinguish right from wrong, good legislation from bad, by calculating the consequences in terms of pleasure and pain if the rule or law were obeyed, and comparing them with the consequences if it were not obeyed or did not exist. But these consequences are envisaged as manifesting themselves either within our own lifetime, or at least within a span of time within which we can more or less foresee how things will be. Those who are supposed to benefit or suffer from the obedience to or breach of the principle are human, not particular humans, but any who may come within the consequential sphere of the acts or omissions in question, in a relatively foreseeable short or medium term. Bentham, it is true, raised the question whether other animals than humans, because they too can suffer pain, should not ideally be brought into the calculation of pleasures and pains. But though he thought that one day our sympathies might be expanded so far, on the whole he was prepared, as a jurist, to concentrate solely on the probable effects of any proposed legislation upon humans. As for J. S. Mill, so far from contemplating extending the calculus of pleasures and pains to include animals other than humans, he held that not even all humans could count for one in the calculations. Infants, for example, should not count; nor should 'savages', by which he meant mostly those who lived in far off lands and of whose culture we had no understanding. Neither Bentham nor Mill could have foreseen a time when we are required to think about what may happen to a world not decades but hundreds or even thousands of years from the present, as a consequence of what we do or neglect to do now. Yet such are the issues faced by 'green' politics, and by anyone who is prepared to be realistic about the future, and to attempt to legislate about environmental issues.

However, Parfit holds that something much more radical is needed than a mere up-date of consequentialist ethics. He believes that as long as we think of our own identity as attaching, as I have argued that it does, to our living bodies which were born on a certain day, and will live a certain length of time and then die, we can never identify with the future, and can therefore never take that kind of responsibility for it that we take for future and foreseeable events in our own lives. He thinks that it is possible, and desirable, that we should change our concept of personal identity. He does not deny that, up to a point, it is right to take a 'reductionist' or 'monistic' line about the nature of the human individual; that is to say, he does not want to return to the Cartesian division between the human body and that which lies inside it, the mind or soul or spirit. Equally he would not, I suppose, deny that if you think of a human as simply a thing among things, then this thing has a purely physical identity, and can be located, relocated, pointed at, in short treated as a single object existing through time and in space, just as any other animal may be. In this sense he would have to agree that an individual human, like an individual robin, has a specific life-span, and comes to an end with death. Nevertheless, as I understand him, he regards it as possible to distinguish this kind of identity, from what he thinks is a more significant psychological identity, namely that experienced 'warmth and familiarity' to use the words of William James, which makes us take responsibility for some at least of the actions of our past selves, and some of their thoughts, and for our projected future selves. Parfit refers to this relation between myself and that for which I take responsibility as 'connectedness'. He suggests that the two important elements, psychologically speaking, in our thought about ourselves are connectedness and continuity. But connectedness and continuity together may hold between me and a number of different future people. Let us imagine, for example, that I have two pupils, with whom I have shared my ideas, and who have taken these ideas over and developed them. I am connected with these two pupils; and the relation of continuity also holds between me and them. This is entailed in the meaning of the word 'pupil'. And I may take responsibility for what they think, whether it turns out well or ill, in so far as I believe I was to a large extent the cause of their thinking as they do, the source of their ideas. And so personal identity, in the new sense of personal responsibility, according to Parfit, must not be thought of as a

narrowly one to one relation (if this makes sense), a relation
which, as it were, confines me to my single identical body. It is
rather a one/many relation, a connectedness between different
phases of a human's physical and psychological life, but holding
equally between one human and many others. Thus, while I
may experience and own to connectedness and continuity (and
thus to identity in the new sense) with my two pupils, I need
own no such relation with phases of my own life which I can
no longer remember. These I may disown, just as much as I
may disown responsibility for the thoughts and actions of other
people, with whom I have had no connection whatever. Physical
continuity, which I have argued to be the fundamental notion
in our idea of personal identity (just as it is fundamental to
the identity over time of any physical object, animate or in-
animate), is, according to Parfit, unimportant. Indeed, he holds
that so to identify myself with a single member of the human
species is both metaphysically naive and morally deplorable.

Parfit gives several hypothetical examples to show the naivety
of the belief that personal identity is essentially bodily identity.
He asks us to imagine my donating my brain to my brother,
and to imagine further that not only the brain but the entire
neural system going with it could be transplanted. In this case,
he argues, my brother becomes me. I no longer exist, but he
is I. Then, secondly, we are to imagine my brain being divided
between two recipients both of whom survive, though of course
I do not. Here there is no answer to the question who is identical with me, as there was in the former case, at least if we
insist that identity is a one/one relation. But given the new
one/many sense of identity, there is nothing wrong with saying
that I am identical with both recipients. Finally, we are asked
to consider the case of my being cloned, so that there are two
people in the world, myself and my replica. If I die while my
replica remains alive, Parfit wants us to say that this is my
survival. Parfit is ambivalent about the force of these arguments, in so far as they are wholly hypothetical, and suggest
things that are impossible. I share this doubt; for our concept
of personal identity is based, naturally, upon what we know to
be possible, upon the way things are. If we consider cases which
are too remote from the real world there may be no interesting
answer to the question how our idea of personal identity would

adapt itself; we can, hypothetically, say whatever we like. However, we know that the cloning of humans is biologically possible, as the transplant of brains and neural systems is not, at least for the foreseeable future. Let us therefore consider only this last example. Is it the case that if there are two people who are clones and one dies the one who has died has survived? I do not believe that this is what we would be inclined to say. If I knew that I had one or more clones I would not believe that I was going to survive my death, any more than I should believe this if I were one of identical twins. Clones are, after all, nothing else than artificially arranged identical twins. That those who did survive would be very like me is irrelevant (though it might irrationally seem quite a nice idea, as I lay on my death-bed). The first reason why the surviving one would not be me is that she would in fact be a different thing from me, as occupying different space from my space. Secondly, even if we were clones, since we would have lived our physically separate lives, we would no longer even be alike in every respect. For any two people even if they shared their lives as clones would develop differently from each other, as their brains made their own mappings of their experience (see chapter 6). Finally, what I will have meant all along when I used the pronoun 'I' was this complete living entity, body-including-brain. Ontologically, the idea of survival is a matter of the continuing life of this living entity; and I in this sense shall have no continuing life. Parfit would take such arguments as evidence of an unregenerate adherence to the idea of personal identity as the identity of a body. And so it is; psychological connectedness is in my view a totally different idea, and cannot be a substitute for that of personal identity. That there will be people other than me in the future who will have thoughts and feelings like mine, even that their thoughts and feelings may be derived in part from mine, does not entail that I survive. It may, however, entail something different: it may mean that I, alive now, am right to be interested in the thoughts and feelings of other people after I am dead. But at this point we move from ontological to moral considerations.

Parfit has a moral point, but makes it differently. He argues that because we are so much locked into regarding ourselves as individuals, single members of the species, who have been born and will die, we tend to limit our responsibility for the consequences of our acts to those cases where singly and separately we have caused something to happen. Thus, I may feel a guilty responsibility if I knowingly left my camp fire burning, and caused a whole forest to catch fire. But there are many cases where what I do individually makes no appreciable difference to the future. It is only if I think of myself as a member of a *kind* of people, or a *generation* of people, that the notion of responsibility can get a grip on what I do. It is therefore morally incumbent on us, according to Parfit, to depersonalize our acts. I personally will not harm the ecological balance of nature if I go out one night and catch a fish. But the society of which I am a member may be guilty of over-fishing and thus of great environmental harm; and I ought to seek my identity not with my past or future individual self, but with this society of which I am, like it or not, a member. I must not confine my ascription of guilt to myself alone, as an individual agent.

Such 'depersonalization' is said to have another consequence. It shows that we need not know to whom we have a duty in order to have it. There need be no exact limit on my duties. It has often been argued, for instance by Mary Midgley (see her *Beast and Man*, Harvester Press, 1979, p. 222), that we cannot have indefinite or infinite duties. For 'ought implies can': it is contradictory to suppose that there could be a duty which I could not fulfil; and if my duty is of infinite, or even indefinite scope, I cannot fulfil it. Parfit thinks differently. I may, as an individual policy-maker, avoid harming existing people if I store nuclear waste on the site of a new power station; but what about those who will be harmed when the short-term safety of the waste comes to an end? Of course, if people do not exist, there will be no one to be harmed; and thus there could be an argument for saying that, since we do not know how many people there will be, or whether indeed there will be any, we just as a matter of duty prefer the claims of those whom we know to exist now. But if, in the Parfit manner, we can depersonalize our way of thinking about consequences, we can grasp the possibility of considering the effects of what we do on people who are unspecified, even who may or may not ever exist, nonsensical as this may sound. Our duty does not derive from ourselves as single individuals; nor is it a duty towards single individuals. It is a duty towards the world as a whole. Some such depersonalized notion has crept into recent UK and European legislation under the heading of 'harm to the environment'. I suspect that perhaps parliamentary draftsmen may not quite have realized what a revolutionary concept this was. For even if, in the legislation that incorporates it, it refers mainly to harm to the present environment, by, for example, the emission of chemical waste into rivers or sewage into the sea, yet it is impossible to think of such harm in terms of the present alone. If waterlands are made uninhabitable for certain species of bird by being drained or polluted, this change will remain for the unforeseeable future. If guillemots are driven away from the offshore of the Shetlands by oil pollution, it is not to be supposed that this change will last for just the present (however the present is defined).

Nowadays we have become accustomed to feeling some responsibility for people who are far distant from us in space. We are shocked by words spoken as short a time ago as 1938 of 'far-distant people of whom we know nothing'. School children are taught, sometimes to the irritation of their parents, to be as much or more concerned with people who live in Africa or Eastern Europe as they are with people who live on their doorstep, or within the door. Parfit argues that we should feel no less responsibility for people who are distant from ourselves in time. It is only our limited notion of ourselves, tied to single human bodies with a beginning and an end, that limits our vision. He calls the normal view, namely that we are less responsible the further distant the future, the 'social discount theory'. And he says:

> Suppose we are considering how to dispose safely of nuclear waste. If we believe in the social discount theory we shall be concerned with safety only in the nearer future. We shall not be troubled by the fact that some nuclear waste will be radioactive for thousands of years. At a discount rate of 5% one death next year counts for more than a billion deaths in 500 years. On this view catastrophe in the future can be counted as morally trivial. (*Reasons and Persons*, p. 356 and Appendix F)

And so he thinks the social discount theory is morally untenable.

I believe that Parfit is here quite unrealistic. Whatever children may be taught at school, and however hard those of us who are not schoolchildren may try, our efforts to treat distant people (unless they are specially related to ourselves) as absolutely on equal terms as far as guilt and compassion go are not generally wholly successful; nor would it be a general good if they were. For our sympathies, as David Hume knew, are limited. But upon them rests all our moral sense. We may try to extend our sympathies, or mitigate the effects of their limitation by moral principles, or by an attempt at Parfit-like 'depersonalization', and the reflection that people, however far away, are also human. But to try too hard would for most of us result in a lessening of those domestic human concerns out of which most of the moral virtues arise. Moreover, we often quite simply do not know enough to enable us to take the best possible steps, or indeed any steps, to alleviate the sufferings of those who are distant from us.

The case of future people is still more difficult to grasp. No one holds the 'social discount' theory as a theory; and certainly no one would be able to put a figure to the discount that is presumed. Nevertheless, we do, and I believe, must think less about the very distant future than the near future simply because of the factor of ignorance, which unlike our ignorance of people who live far away, is irremediable. We need an effort of imagination to envisage the past. But we can learn to do so because if we apply our minds to the past, even the impersonal 'indefinite' past, we can usually uncover some evidence which can be interpreted as a foundation for our reconstructions. But there is little that can serve as evidence for the future. The situation is not parallel, in any case. We can perhaps hope to discover and relive the past. We can even reinterpret it. We can regret it, and in certain cases repent in so far as we personally have been responsible for what has happened. But we cannot change it. We can change the future, and thus we can feel anxiety about the future, in a way that we cannot about the past. But there is always a temptation to shrug off this anxiety, by saying 'It will last my time'. This is the attitude which Parfit wants us to abandon by thinking of ourselves as literally part of the future, surviving into it, and living in it, in a newly invented sense.

Parfit is wrong, I think, to suppose that we could not feel such guilt or responsibility about the future unless we were somehow conceptually and psychologically linked with it. As I have argued, he tries to forge this link by urging us to change our views, so as to embrace a weaker form of personal identity than that founded on our own individual life and death. I hold, however, that we can assert our continuity with the future without any such radical change in our ideas. But it is difficult to do, and tempting to omit. In this way it is like the obligation Christianity used to lay on people to repent before it was too late, and think of the Life of the World to Come, rather than always only of this present life. In both cases immediate sacrifices were called for, or the postponement of instant gratification, for the sake of a future good, or at least the mitigation of a future evil. But now this good or this evil will not, we know, affect ourselves. We can interest ourselves in it only by reflecting that those who suffer or who benefit will be, like us, human. They will then be in the same boat that we now are in; in this sense humanity is, as a whole, all in the boat together, regardless of time. The crucial factor here is that we, being human, are unique in being able to think in these terms. No other animals are able to envisage even a future that is immediate and concerns themselves, still less an indefinite future, a future of the world as a whole. And this ability creates an obligation. If we can think in this way, and feel these anxieties, and if we are the only creatures who can, and if the thoughts and the anxieties dictate certain kinds of behaviour (not wasting natural resources, for example) then they seem to generate moral imperatives.

There is no radically new moral concept involved here. Morality has always arisen out of sympathy and unselfishness, and the power to imagine the future for others as well as for ourselves. These factors have given rise both to moral virtues, habits that is, of behaving in ways that seem to be likely to be beneficial rather than harmful, and also to moral principles, general rules that seem likely to produce good rather than harm, in general, if obeyed. The only new factor is that we have now more technology by means of which we can do harm, as well as good; and a bit more knowledge, enabling us to make better forecasts of the long-term effects of what we do. In the nineteenth century there were a few prophets, such as Blake, who saw the possible long-term effects of technology; and saw how the whole universe was one. In the eyes of these prophets we do, as humans, have a general obligation towards and responsibility for the future.

However, there are those who argue that we can have no obligation towards future generations because we cannot know what they will want or need. If they exist at all, they will be alien creatures. But, against this, Gregory Kavka suggests, rightly in my view, that, though we may not know in detail what these future people may want, we can know what they will need, simply on the basis of their humanity. They will need to eat and drink and breathe breathable air; they will need shelter and security and health (and these things embrace much that they will want as well as need). (See Kavka's 'The Futurity Problem' in *Obligations to Future Generations*, ed. R. I. Sikora and Brian Barry, Philadelphia University Press, 1978, pp. 93–110). Our sympathy with future humans is the basis of our obligations to them, as it is of all our obligations. As Robin Attwood puts it: 'Our obligations to people are not lessened by the mere fact of their futurity' (Attwood, *The Ethics of Environmental Concern*, University of Georgia Press, 1963, p. 950).

I have suggested that we cannot claim to have no obligations to the future by reason of ignorance. Even if it is true that those who in the nineteenth century built huge industrial plants and slums to go with them were ignorant of the long-term effects on people that these would have, and saw no further than the rise in prosperity that would follow for themselves and others like them, we cannot claim such ignorance. And if we are not ignorant, morality demands that we should not be indifferent either. There are aspects of the future about which we are truly ignorant, however; and here we have, in my view, the negative obligation of caution. There is an obvious sense in which, without changing our view of personal identity, or performing any other metaphysical feat, we can understand ourselves to be part and parcel with the future, and that is through our genes. It is, or will soon be, within our power to manipulate human genes in such a way as to change the human gene pool for ever.

This would come about if defective genes were detected in human sperm or eggs, or in a very early embryo in which the genes were not yet differentiated (before 14 days from fertilization) and if these genes were removed, or others added to them. Such therapeutic manipulation would be known as germ-line gene therapy, and the effects would be not merely on the child that was born as an immediate result of the fertilization, but on all of the descendants of that child. At the present time much work is being done in the field of gene therapy for the cure of specific genetic diseases (such as cystic fibrosis, or Duchesne's muscular dystrophy) but the procedures when they are available will be used only on older foetuses or children who have been born, through surgery or genetically manipulated drugs, and only on specific cells, such that the effects of the gene manipulation will be confined to the child who has been treated. Such procedures are known as somatic-cell gene therapy. There is a general agreement among a majority of the medical profession, not just in this country but in Europe, the USA and Australia, that germ-line gene therapy shall not be attempted, though this is by no means universally agreed in theory. There are various arguments against such attempts. One is the so-called slippery slope argument, namely that such therapy would not be confined to the search for the eradication of monogenetic diseases for which there is no cure, but would spread to the enhancement of characteristics deemed to be desirable, or the elimination of such undesirable traits as aggression or stupidity. Such arguments are based not so much on logic as on a particular view of human nature – that people will always want to go further, or acquire more than they have got. They are persuasive because of the fears they play on, concerned with the apparent possibility of changing human characteristics one by one.

The better argument against germ-line genetic manipulation is, however, the argument from ignorance. Knowledge of disease genes, and why it is that some persist in populations at greater frequencies than others, is extremely limited; therefore it is impossible to be certain that an attempt to eradicate these disease genes for ever would be of long-term benefit to future generations. The best-known example of the kind of side-effect, if it may be so called, of certain genes is that of the gene for sickle-cell anaemia. This gene is particularly prevalent in tropical Africa and the Mediterranean. It is now known that the gene protects carriers (that is, those who have one disease gene and one normal gene of a pair) from malaria. Thus, carriers had in the past a survival advantage both over those who had normal genes, and over those who had two disease genes; the former being liable to die of malaria, the latter to die of sickle-cell anaemia. Because of this advantage, carriers were more likely to survive and have children, and thus the sickle-cell anaemia gene was perpetuated. If that gene had been able to be eradicated in the past, the advantages that it conferred would also have been lost. At the present time, when the malarial mosquito is less prevalent, this genetic advantage is not as relevant as it was. Nevertheless, the example shows that harm might be done, of a so far unpredictable kind, by any deliberate alteration of the gene pool. Genes which cause harm in one environment may have unforeseen evolutionary advantages in other environments. We have a duty, then, to future humans not to press ahead with manipulation of germ-line genes.

I am not myself convinced that there will ever come a time when we should embark on such a programme, even if the gains (let us say the elimination of AIDS) seemed to be enormous. Even if the extreme difficulties of such procedures were to be lessened, and thus the probability of human error also diminished (and any error would be perpetuated from one generation to another) I still think that our ignorance of the future is and will remain too profound. I have spoken so far of ignorance only in the context of human gene manipulation, and have argued that ignorance imposes on us a duty of caution. The same sort of argument can of course be applied to the genetic manipulation of animals other than humans, and of plants. Here, because there is a greater possibility of experiment, it is possible to make better ecological predictions. Even so, any genetically modified animal or plant, any genetically engineered microbe or virus, needs to be monitored. Above all, the effects of genetic engineering need to be considered as far as possible with an eye not to immediate gain (agricultural or industrial) but to the foreseeable future of the environment as a whole.

I have mentioned already the concept of Harm to the Environment which is now incorporated in UK environmental law.

And it seems to me plain that we increasingly perceive a duty not just to future humans, not even just to those aspects of the natural world from which humans will obviously benefit or from the absence of which they will suffer, but to the preservation of the natural world as a whole. Moral philosophers have recently occupied themselves quite busily with the idea of such a duty of care for the future of the world. Some who hold that if I have a duty then something to which I have a duty must have a right, have even invented the notion of the rights of the environment (and of course, notoriously, the rights of animals). Others have spoken of the interest, of animals or of the environment. I do not believe that such contortions of common sense or legal reality are necessary. But it is necessary to consider why it is that many of us do feel ourselves to have this sort of duty. In discussing this question, I want to lay on one side, as far as possible, considerations such as those I have been concerned with in talking about genetic engineering. I do not want to consider issues of what will or will not benefit food production or fuel supplies for future humans. Neither do I want to consider what it is necessary to do in order to secure health and safety for ourselves and our successors. I want to consider the different and perhaps more obscure question of why we feel ourselves to have a duty not to allow species of plants and animals to become extinct; or why we want certain features of the natural world, mountains, rivers, beaches, let us say, to continue to exist unexploited and unspoilt. The first, and in a way, the only answer to this question must be that we want these things to continue to exist because we value them. Not only so, but we regard them as intrinsically valuable. This may seem blindingly obvious; but it is in fact quite a difficult thought to understand. Concern for the environment has become such a taken-for-granted way of displaying virtue that generally it is only politicians and legislators who have to think of the justifications for this expensive hobby. How much are we prepared to pay? What precisely do we want to conserve, and why?

The acute difficulty of weighing up comparative costs, or of estimating value for money in ordinary cost-benefit terms, arises from the fact that the values involved here are genuinely and ineradicably sentimental; that is to say, they arise from our aesthetic, moral and religious sentiments. We want people to experience these sentiments. We generally believe that the world would be a worse place if no one experienced them. But it is difficult to say that they are worth just so much of the gross national income. To regard something as intrinsically valuable is to value it for itself, not for its consequences, or as a means to some different and valuable end. We are sometimes inhibited about declaring that things are good in themselves, or of intrinsic value, because of a fear that we may be expressing merely our own feelings about them, and because of an obscure feeling that such language should perhaps be used only of moral goods. We are, knowingly or unknowingly, profoundly influenced by Kant's view that the only thing valuable in itself is the good will, that is the rational source of all moral principles, and something peculiar, therefore, to humans. Humans are by their very ability to form such principles set apart from the rest of nature, which must, it seems, be valued only as instrumental, as a means to human ends. It is this obscure belief which leads to the use of the dismal word 'amenity', by Rural District Councils and economists, to designate valued features of the country such as clean beaches or unspoiled moorlands or wetlands where birds can breed. Even species of birds and animals are thought of as 'amenities'. And 'amenity' in its current sense means 'a useful and pleasant service', for example a municipal swimming pool, or tennis courts. It is inextricably connected with that other municipal word, 'leisure'. Now we may all accept that some money must be spent on leisure amenities; but once we start using this kind of language for the natural world and all that is in it, we seem to have changed the subject, to say nothing of having reduced the world to a kind of park or garden.

How then are we to think and talk about our duty to be aware of and look after the natural world, for its own sake? How are we to explain to ourselves and those responsible for policy (and largely for money to be spent on policy) that it has been a wrong to allow the corncrake to become virtually extinct, or the skylark and the peewit to become rarities on the downland where they used to flourish? It must be conceded to speak of these features of the world as valuable, even as intrinsically valuable, entails our looking at them from a human point of view. We have no other point of view available to us. Moreover, if there were no humans in the world to value things it is certain that there would be nothing valuable. To think otherwise, when we think of a world without people, is sur-reptitiously to insert a human observer into the picture. But that humans are needed for things to be valuable does not entail that things are valuable only in so far as they are service-able or useful or even pleasant to humans (in short, that they are 'amenities'). We may value things precisely because they are not such as to be subdued or dominated by humans. We may feel a duty not to allow them to be spoiled, or to disappear from the world, just because they are not our possessions, over which we have the right, if we so wish, to commit them to the flames or the jumble sale.

There is a long tradition in Judaeo-Christian thought which is the tradition of stewardship. This can be traced back to the Old Testament, particularly in the idea of dominion. Man was put in dominion over nature according to the myth of the crea-tion, but that dominion was like kingship; it carried with it the duty to care for that over which you had dominion. Admittedly, this tradition was variously interpreted. But the idea familiar from the Psalms, that God is creator of the whole world and that all God's creatures are equally evidence of his power and glory, led to many Christians, from the early Fathers onwards, adopting the notion that men were stewards of the whole of nature, bearing a responsibility to plants and animals in virtue of the position of superiority that God had given them. And this is, after all, only a metaphorical way of asserting the truth we have already recognized, and taken into account, namely that only humans can envisage the whole earth, and all that therein is. Only they can think of how things originated and how they will survive into the future. No one can deny that, in this respect if in no other (that is, in respect of their imagination and their language), humans are better endowed than other animals. But their being able to conceive things in this light, *sub specie aeternitatis*, gives them a duty to take care of what they find, and not to be wantonly destructive, or cause fruitless harm. The idea of stewardship is a useful and effective metaphor of what, on grounds of what we value, we may well believe to be the truth. Those who are prepared to use this metaphor find it is illuminating: it sheds light on the position that humans actually occupy in the world, as well as their sense of what this position entails.

At a conference held in Oxford in 1991, Professor Bernard Williams read a paper in which he raised questions about the nature of the values at issue in environmental discussion (Williams, 'Must concern for the environment be centred on human beings?' in *Ethics and the Environment*, Bocardo Press, 1992, pp. 60–8). In this paper he spoke of two crucial issues. One is our concept of the Natural. He argued, rightly, that we often claim to want to conserve 'nature', or to protect it from further human erosion. Yet when we look around us, almost everything we see has been manipulated and changed by human intervention. There is a danger that we may claim that, for example, some aspects of landscape should be conserved exactly as they are, when two or three hundred years ago, to say nothing of a thousand years ago, these landscapes would not have existed. The very concept of 'landscape' is an aesthetic concept, just as the eighteenth and nineteenth-century idea of a 'prospect' was aesthetic. The progress of nature into art is a long one, and we cannot cut off at any stage and deem this to be natural, that artificial. The whole notion of looking at nature, or enjoying it, is fraught with difficulties, involving as it does a certain elitism, a class division between those whom we wish to allow to enjoy these pleasures, those we wish to exclude, and those whom we may permit to enjoy the pleasures in a more 'peasant-like' way, as they go to work on their farms. We are in danger of reintroducing the concept of the 'amenity', even if we would avoid the word.

His second point was that, in addition to the pleasure and the sense of peace that humans may get from the contemplation of nature, there is also another basic reaction to nature. This is a reaction of fear or awe. He says:

> Our sense of restraint in the face of nature, a sense very basic to conservation concerns, will be grounded in a form of fear; a fear not just of the power of nature itself, but what might be called Promethean Fear, a fear of taking too lightly or inconsiderately our relations with nature. On this showing... the grounds of our attitudes will not be an extension of benevolence or altruism...it will be based rather on a sense of an

opposition between ourselves and nature, as an old, unbounded
and potentially dangerous enemy which requires respect. 'Respect'
is the notion that perhaps more than any other needs examination here, and not first in the sense of respect for a sovereign,
but that in which we have a healthy respect for mountainous
terrain or treacherous seas. (*Ethics and the Environment*, p. 67)

I believe that this is a very important observation, and one
often omitted in the consideration of the grounds on which
our valuing of the natural environment is based. We are here
confronted with ideas very like those ideas of the sublime which
I earlier quoted from Kant. The sublime is the unbounded. It
is that which we do not and cannot wholly grasp or tame.
Above all, the sublime objects of nature are everlasting. They
are in opposition to ourselves not just in the sense that they
may be our enemy, but that they stand for something which
we can never achieve, that is for eternity. We can use them as
symbols, therefore, for that which we can never otherwise
express, our sense of immortality. We can share in the eternity
of these natural objects, in that they can provide us with the
idea of continuity between ourselves and the world as it was
and the world as it will be. I do not believe therefore that we
need change our concept of personal identity in the way that
Derek Parfit invites us to do in order to interest ourselves in
the future of the world. The value that we attach to the natural
world, whether we think of it as the handiwork of God or
otherwise, is connected with the value we attach to the everlasting. The more we are aware of ourselves as individuals with
a limited life-span, members of a species of animal, though with
unique powers to conceive of the grandeurs of nature of which
we are a part, the more highly we will value that which will
outlast us, and the more strongly we may sense it to be our
duty not knowingly to despoil it. It is in this way that we feel
ourselves responsible for the future, recognizing that what we
do now, how we behave, makes a difference to how things will
be in the world to come, from everlasting to everlasting. What
we value in the natural world goes further than, and is different
from, the value we attach to other humans, whether present or
future. Such a value is of an intrinsic good, and it is from this
perception that our duty derives.

9

Consequences

At the end of his strange book *Speculum Mentis* R. G. Collingwood wrote this:

> A mind which knows its own changes is by that lifted above
> change. History, and the same is true of memory...is the mind's
> triumph over time. It is a common-place of philosophy that
> whereas sensation is temporal, thought is eternal or extra-
> temporal. Sensation apprehends the here and now, thought ap-
> prehends the everywhere and the always. Hence the abstract
> psychology which splits the mind up into a sensitive and an
> intellectual faculty paradoxically presents us with a picture of
> man as standing with one foot in time, the other in eternity.
> This is mythology, but it is true mythology. (*Speculum Mentis or
> the map of Knowledge*, Oxford University Press, 1924, p. 301)

It has been my concern to argue that it is imagination that
performs the trick of connecting the momentary and ephemeral
with the permanent, the particular with the universal, enabling man to stand with his feet so far astride. I want now to
say something more about the way this function of the imagination relates to a system of values, and the practical consequences such a relation may have. I tried to show that our
individuality, that is our consciousness of being, each one, a
separate centre of experience with a life of our own to lead, is
connected essentially with our ability to think of our own past,
and, to a lesser extent, our own future. We know that we are
continuous with the past; we feel that we are continuous with
what we can foresee and take responsibility for in the future.
This knowledge of continuity, I suggested, derives from what

we may properly call imagination, without which we would be stuck, if conscious at all, firmly in the present. But imagination, and memory which is an aspect of it, depends on our being physical and biological entities, things which persist for a certain time, among other things in the world. For our recollections, and all that we learn and know, are causally connected with our having been in the world to learn them. To speak of a memory of the past implies a continuity of existence, I then being physically continuous with I now, possessed of the same developing brain. In all instances of knowledge, then, in all language-using and all recollecting we are implicitly asserting our physical continuity with the past. However, the past, as I have observed, is not over and done with; our past determines how we interpret the present, in the light of the values we ascribe to things, and how we conceive of the future. These human features, our imagination, our memory and our value-system cannot be prised apart; neither can they be separated from our physical existence in time and space.

We value our sense of continuity not only because we value ourselves, and depend on a kind of self-esteem if we are to live satisfactory lives, but also because there is a sense in which, in apprehending our own individual continuity, we come to be aware of something more general, more universal, more impervious to time than our individual selves. We know very well that we are mortal, but the sense of continuity we each have with both past and future carries within it nevertheless an obscure feeling of eternity, or timelessness. It may well be that one could ascribe some such sense to animals other than humans. The difference is that they cannot tell us about it or compel us to share those symbols which reflect their experienced continuity, nor the way they feel that the story of their lives fits in with the story of the universe. Only we, through language and other representations, can deliberately transform the momentary into the timeless.

This sense of timelessness is related to the belief that some at least of the values we ascribe to things are shared by others and are non-instrumental. We are aware of intrinsic and permanent values, which is to say that some aspects of the world, apprehended perhaps through symbols, or enunciated in stories, are intrinsically significant to us.

The word 'significant' is one we feel readily inclined to use in such contexts as that of Proust's recollections, and his determination to write them down, in the form of the 'one true book', or the search that Coleridge made for natural symbols. It is, though convenient, in a way a fraudulent word, or at least one liable to allow us to get away with something less than clarity. Let us consider for a moment what it means. Something that is significant is something that has meaning. Thus, a mark on a stone may be either significant or non-significant. It may either be a letter (or other sign); or on the other hand it may be a chance mark, produced by accident, or made as mere decoration. This is one meaning of 'significant'. A related meaning is that what is so described is of importance. Thus, a significant victory is a victory that will make a difference to the future course of the war; it is not trivial. It is a victory that is worth winning. And thus, from the idea of meaning, we move to the idea of value. Now we would all agree that there may be things that are of importance to me and to no one else. Even if I can explain to you why something is important to me, for instance how it fits in with my plans as nothing else would, I do not expect that you, though you may understand me, will necessarily also think the thing important. And so it might be that if some aspects of recalling the past are important to me, even give me joy because of their importance, or give me particular terror, this might well be a part of my private life which held no interest for anyone else, except perhaps as a curiosity. But both 'meaning' and, I believe, 'value', have an implicit generality as part of their sense. If I claim that a word or other sign has meaning, then, even if I am the only person who at present understands this word, I must be able to explain to you what it means. A symbol, even though at a particular time it is held to be symbolic of something, to mean it, only by me, must in principle be capable of being understood as symbolic by other people as well. This publicity, this potentially shared sense, is part of what being a word or a sign or a symbol is. And the idea of value shares this feature. It is perfectly true that I may value something highly, or may reject it very strongly, on a scale or according to criteria which are wholly idiosyncratic. But I must be prepared, at least if challenged, to try to get others to share my views. If I say that something is lovable or hateful, beautiful or ugly, good or bad, I am using a language which 'demands assent'. It 'claims the agreement of everyone' in Kant's words, 'just as if it were objective' (*Critique of Judgement*, sec. 32, p. 136). In ascribing these value-characteristics to a thing I show thereby that I expect to be able to explain my way of seeing the thing, and of estimating it, to others besides myself. Thus, in the sense of the word 'significant' there are two elements, that of meaning and that of value, both of which carry with them an implicit universality or at least generality, over and above the idea of importance, which, I have suggested, may be wholly personal.

It is doubtless true that both 'meaning' and 'value' may be used, weakly, in contexts where nothing but a private attitude or understanding is implied. Thus, someone might say that an object or a place 'means a lot to me', and would not expect that it would mean anything to anyone else. Likewise, he might say of the same object 'I value it highly', and in the same way could confine the value to himself alone. All the same, save when qualified by a definite restriction to the first person, the words 'meaningful' and 'valuable' contain a generalizing sense. 'Meaningful' means 'capable of being understood'; and 'valuable' means 'fit to be valued' by anyone.

In the case of values, I have already argued that there are those things which we deem fit to be valued for their own sake, not as a means to anything else. Thus, if we were asked why we valued health, for example, we might have to say simply that we and many other people did so, not because it led to anything or was a means to anything but simply because we would rather it existed than not. It enhances everything. We need not always be able to answer the question 'what do you value it for?' In a somewhat similar way (though I would not claim that the analogy was exact) it seems that there are certain objects which simply do seem to mean something or to suggest something other than themselves. These are what I have spoken of as 'natural symbols'. We can recognize them as having a meaning, without necessarily being able to say what that meaning is. Nevertheless, the attempt to explain, to translate, to interpret is a large part of what literature (and perhaps some of philosophy) is concerned with.

So it is that writers such as Proust, or indeed Wordsworth, believed that if they could get us to understand an experience which is significant to them, they would have achieved something permanent, which would be resistant to, or victorious over, time. For meanings and values, being in the public domain, are necessarily potentially permanent. If I and a number of other people can grasp a meaning or embrace a value, then it is open to us to pass this meaning down to others. Our imagination makes us capable of sympathy with others. It produces in us the notion that we are all in the same boat. And the boat we are in not only contains a lot of people now; it contains past people and, more importantly, future people as well. This is the nature of the triumph over time. It is the belief in human sympathy which alone makes an attempt to tell the truth, such as Proust's, intelligible. It is worth trying to get things right, to make other people understand, not because it will do them good, or save them from error, or help them to avoid mistakes, but simply because this kind of understanding is of intrinsic worth, and links members of the human species together in perpetuity.

If, by the exercise of imagination, we may reach a common understanding of the values we can claim to share with other humans, then the handing on of these values to a new generation must be something of central importance. Values do not simply occur, picked out of the air. Though based on common experiences, the nice and the nasty alike, they must be reflected upon and taught, if they are to become part of the life of the individual, capable of giving meaning to that life. This is most obviously true of moral values, for children, though capable of affection, are not, untaught, prone to behave well in circumstances where this involves sacrificing their immediate wishes; and many children have the instincts of a bully, which they have to be taught to control. And there are other values, things which a child may learn to enjoy and appreciate, to admire and emulate, only if he is taught.

I have argued that the imagination is crucial in the acceptance of shared and continuing values. It is not surprising, therefore, that I would also argue that the education of the imagination is by far the most important educational goal, and that which should be central in any curriculum decisions. With this in mind, I would suggest that the teaching of history is perhaps the most important part of education, a judgement based on the epistemological status of history itself. For the study of history essentially brings us into contact with human motivation, and human capacity, and with the changes people have sought to bring about, for good or ill. And education must aim to make children conscious of their own powers and capacities, raising questions about their freedom to make decisions, and the consequences these decisions may have. They must learn that the past has brought them to where they are, and that it is for them to determine, to a greater or lesser extent, what the future will he. They must learn the lesson of human responsibility. Such educational goals are practical rather than purely academic, as I believe the goals of education should be. By 'practical', I mean not so much that in achieving such goals children will become better able to perform certain specific tasks; it is rather that, the nearer these goals are to being achieved, the better prepared a child will be to lead a critical, intelligent life when he approaches adulthood, being not a mere passenger in society, but an active member, with a sense of direction. The greatest enemy of imagination is to be locked in the present. It is easy for everyone, but especially for children, to think that things have always been as they are now, and that at the moment of our coming into the world and becoming conscious of it, all institutions, all customs, all scientific theories, all standards of taste and behaviour, were immutably fixed. The realization that things have not always been as they are, but that institutions and customs and beliefs have changed and developed over time, is the first requirement for understanding both how things now are, and how they may perhaps be changed in the future. Historical understanding is thus at the centre of all understanding, including the understanding of the sciences. It is only through the recognition of how the concepts we now take for granted have arisen out of what went before that we can become able to delineate the framework of thought within which we operate, to examine critically our dogmatic assumptions. I therefore regard the teaching of history as central to education, and in this teaching I would include some awareness of the history of science and mathematics, of literature, journalism, music and the visual arts, as well as what is most generally regarded as the appropriate subject-matter of history lessons. I believe that the current insistence on the primacy of problem-solving in education may lead to a marginalizing of what ought to be at the centre, the imaginative grasp of the continuity of history.

There is a further aspect of the teaching of history which should place it centrally in any educational curriculum. In the course of such teaching it is inevitable that concepts of moral value will be introduced. Whatever some have alleged, no history teacher is concerned only with 'dates and facts'. Obviously the knowledge of what are accepted facts must be the foundation for more speculative considerations; but in the course of examining and perhaps seeking to establish the facts, questions not only about motivation but about morals must inevitably arise. Was the First World War morally justified? Is there such a thing as a just war? Is assassination ever a good act? What was the real motive behind the crusades? At every stage such questions must be asked, and the teacher must give guidance in answering them. The teacher has to steer a course between dogmatism and relativism. He must say, as honestly as he is able, 'There are differing views about this; but my personal view is such and such'. It is of the greatest possible importance to children that they should learn early, and by example, both that there are different and incompatible value-judgements which may be sincerely arrived at, and that, in this apparently bewildering choice of values, it is possible to adopt a firm and steady point of view, and justify it. A teacher should not expect to get away with simply stating what he thinks. He should be prepared to argue for it, by placing it in the context of other values that he adheres to, and he should also be prepared to have these values questioned. Through this kind of dialogue, pupils will learn both that moral views sometimes differ, but that it is nevertheless possible to conceive of and uphold ideals which may be understood and shared. It is this lesson, to be learned nowhere better than in a school history class, which will make possible a kind of convergence or consensus of values outside the classroom without which a society will become ungovernable.

The narrative of history is constantly interpreted and reinterpreted to reveal values. What makes this crucial to the developing awareness of children is that the narrative is not closed. The past is continuous with the present. Just as, for an individual, his memory shapes what he is now, so, in the public domain, history makes us, the living, what we are, and gives us the understanding that may help to shape the future. Our sense of this, our historical imagination, separates us from other animals. It is only humans who can place themselves in a continuous moral context, in which values, what is liked and disliked, feared, admired or despised, can be articulated and handed on, not simply through the genes, nor even only by example, but by discussion and dialogue, by established trust and benevolent influence. It is through this kind of articulated value-system that humans can come to regard their lives as having significance.

I shall return to the question of consensus in a moment, in its generally political sense. First, however, it is necessary to explore a little further the sense in which values must be shared. That there exist more people than one is, obviously, a fact central to the idea of morality. On a desert island with no hope of escape the castaway would be released from morality. If he set himself rules of life, these would not give rise to moral imperatives (though they might feel like this if he were tempted to neglect them). The rules would have arisen only from the idea that he would rather be one sort of person than another, that he would rather clean his teeth, say, or learn how to do things than lie about in squalor and idleness. The issue of good or harm to oneself alone could not ever have given rise to the concept of morals. If we sometimes seem to incorporate such an idea within the sphere of morality, this is an idea borrowed from the public world, where moral ideas had their origin and have their proper use. Not only does morality involve our relations with others, however, but it is, and has always been recognized by philosophers as being, social in the sense of involving common values, and a common good. The two things naturally go together. This recognized fact leads to the question whether some shared assertions of value, or some interpretations of what is good and what is bad, can amount to true assertions or interpretations. This is a form of the question that has been raised in various forms in the preceding pages. We may raise it here by asking whether some things are absolutely worth more than others, or are absolutely better. David Wiggins, in his book *Needs Values and Truth* (Blackwell, 1987, p. 87), suggests that when people ask, as they sometimes do, whether life has any point or meaning this is often what they are really asking.

There is no doubt that we, most of us, want our lives to have what I have spoken of as significance, what Wiggins speaks of as meaning; that is, we want somehow to be able to locate a value in what we do or think which is both intelligible to others and important to ourselves, out of which, even if not at an elevated level, we may experience the Joy which Coleridge lost in his dejection, and Proust had not found until he embarked on the great project of writing the 'only true book'. And, I must emphasize, the value that we want to locate need not necessarily be a specifically moral value. If we discover something that we find intrinsically worth doing, for its own sake, such as playing a musical instrument, or gardening, then this may be the source of the sought-for imaginative Joy.

But we may be told that it is not enough to want this. We ought not to pretend that there are permanent and objective values to which we can try to conform our wills or which we can state in true propositions, if there can be none. (Such objections have mostly been raised, understandably enough, with regard to the search for permanent and timeless moral values. It may seem a matter of less concern whether or not someone believes that there is an absolute sense in which music or gardening are worthwhile and can give meaning to life.) According to such arguments, it would have been easy to say what was the meaning or purpose of your life, and to say what, within that life, you ought or ought not to do, if you believed that God had placed you in the world with certain ends in view, and even given you a certain station in life which carried specific duties with it. Your station and its duties could then be laid out in a series of true statements. Moreover, if you could add to this the belief that if you failed in your duties you would suffer eternal damnation, and if you succeeded you would be rewarded with everlasting bliss, your life would be both meaningful and motivated. It has been powerfully argued, for example by J. L. Mackie (in *Ethics: Inventing Right and Wrong*, Penguin Books, 1977), that the objective-sounding language of morals, especially the language of duties and obligations, is nothing but a left-over from the days of such literal belief. We invent morality and prop up our invention with linguistic devices suggestive of certainty and of matters of fact, to give ourselves the security of a sense of purpose in our lives. We cannot bear to seem to be doing things that are pointless, and so we tell ourselves stories which give our activities and our life as a whole a meaning. There is a curious discussion of the question of the meaning of life in a book by Richard Taylor (*Good and Evil*, Macmillan, 1970). This account of the matter is discussed by Wiggins (*Needs, Values and Truth*, Essay III, pp. 92–103). Taylor raises the question by retelling the story of Sisyphus, condemned by the gods to roll a stone to the top of a hill whence it immediately rolls down again, and he has to roll it up, and so on for ever. Taylor says that viewed from without, this is objectively speaking a totally meaningless or pointless life. He says that if Sisyphus were trying to roll stones up in order to build a beautiful temple at the top of the hill, then at first sight it might seem that there was more point to his life, hard though it might be. (I am not sure whether he is allowed in this version occasionally to succeed in getting a stone to the top or not.) But Taylor argues that even with the temple as his goal, his life would still be objectively futile, or meaningless, because the temple would not last for ever. He holds that if the life of Sisyphus or of anyone else is to have meaning we must contrast objective with subjective meaning, and say that a man's life can have only the meaning that he himself gives it, whatever he achieves or fails to achieve. If the gods in mitigation of his punishment had given Sisyphus a drug which caused him to want to do what he had to do, then his life would have been subjectively full of satisfaction, and so he would have said it had meaning, and we could have said so too, if we had adopted his point of view. Taylor concludes that the meaning of life is within us, it is not bestowed from outside. And he adds that 'it far exceeds in its beauty and permanence any heaven of which men have ever dreamed or yearned for.' He holds that all animals could be said to have meaningful lives if we could see things through their eyes, provided only that what they want to do, what they are as it were programmed to do, is not frustrated.

Taylor seems to me to make three mistakes in this argument. First, he appears to hold that if what I do will have an outcome which will not last literally for ever, then it is objectively futile to do it. This would mean that all works of art, all literature, all music, to say nothing of all cooking or gardening, is 'objectively' meaningless. As I have already argued, we do not need to believe that the world will last literally for ever in order to be able to contrast what is eternal with what will last for a day. A temple might well last a very long time, by all ordinary human standards, and certainly longer than the life of a man. So if the temple was beautiful, or useful, it would not be a futile act to build it, even if one day in the distant future it will fall into ruins. The idea of the useful in itself is perfectly 'objective', and may often be the answer to the question whether there is any meaning or point in an activity. That a bird has to build a new nest every year, or generally does so, does not entail that its building the nest this year is meaningless.

Secondly, Taylor confuses what I have called significance, and he calls 'meaning', with happiness, or contentment. There may well be satisfaction of a kind, but neither happiness nor contentment in a life lived according to some self-imposed discipline, a determination, for example, to look after a disabled child, rather than let him be institutionalized, or a commitment to pursuing an aesthetic goal. The person who lived such a life would be able to say what the point of life was; but might nevertheless be profoundly discontented. Thirdly, and even more important, in his supposition that all animals, from their own point of view, live meaningful lives, he fails to take into account the difference between men and other animals. For it is only because they possess imagination, and can construct ideals for themselves of how they would like their lives to be, what they would like to achieve, how they would like their life's work to affect people other than themselves, both immediately and in the future, that humans are able to reflect that their lives are either meaningful or meaningless. Without such an ability to think beyond the present the concept of the significant or meaningful has no application. Whatever efforts we might make to see things through the eyes of other animals, what we would not find, without anthropomorphism, is the concept of a moral ideal, or of any other generalized value. We could understand what these other animals want; and we can understand what they need. But such wants and needs will be necessarily experienced by them as attached only to the here and now. *We* may generalize our wants and needs, even turn them into ideals. *They* cannot. The idea of morality is one of the ways, and probably the most important, in which humans in fact generalize their wants, wishes and, what they have and other animals do not, their aspirations.

If we speak of someone's having aspirations, we mean that he adopts a value or an ideal which may be forever beyond his powers, but which will act as a goal, and may give purpose to his life. His purpose may not be particularly good nor particularly elevated. His aspirations may be to climb up the social ladder, to get rich, or to grow bigger onions than his neighbours. But to conceive of these ambitions is a function of imagination, and it is certainly in terms of imagined ideals that humans may regard their lives as worth or not worth living. The building of the beautiful temple in the revised Sisyphus myth was an aspiration. The thought that the temple would be beautiful, or useful, or a fit honour for the gods is, as I argued, enough to make the life of trying to build it significant. It does not have to be the case that the temple will last literally for ever, although the relatively permanent nature of the temple is commonly an element in making its building seem worth doing.

Moral ideals, if they are such as to make the pursuit of them absolutely worthwhile, must, more than temples, be thought to have permanence. It is not necessary for us to invent an external validation or authority for the ideals we adopt in order that we may be committed to them. But it is necessary, I would argue, to believe that they have a value beyond the merely personal; and that, as they have been derived from ideals exemplified in the past, so they will be exemplified in the future, or so we hope, by others than ourselves. They must be thought of as values which persist, and will continue to be upheld, if not for ever, then for far beyond the present moment. As I have argued, a moral value necessarily involves the thought of others besides myself for whom it is a value. To adopt such a shared value is to give to life a significance which could in principle be shared, precisely because something that is in this manner social has an existence beyond one's own temporal and spatial limits. It gives significance to life 'to adopt', as Wiggins puts it, 'a point of view that can be shared between the members of an actual society, to give expression to a potentially enduring and transmissable shared sensibility' (David Wiggins, ibid., Essay II, p. 66).

This brings us back to the question of moral consensus which, in one form or another, seems to me to be a central political issue, especially in a society which, we are constantly assured, is essentially 'plural'. It is cosy and agreeable to live among people who share sensibilities of other kinds, who, for example, share tastes in art, music, food and, generally, what is enjoyable and funny. We may choose our friends from among those with whom we might claim consensus on such matters. But such comfortable arrangements are no more, themselves, than a matter of taste. There appear to be some people who positively revel in living among others with whom they disagree on all such matters of taste. In matters of morality, however, disagreement appears to have more serious consequences. A radical absence of consensus may, as I have suggested, lead to a breakdown of society, a condition of anarchy which would be worse than just uncomfortable.

It may be argued that to suppose a consensus morality to be necessary to society is radically mistaken. For one of the most important lessons we have learned over the centuries is the lesson of tolerance, and especially religious tolerance. Since many of the most deeply held moral beliefs are related to religion, either arising directly from a genuine faith, or indirectly from once-held beliefs, it cannot be right to suggest that we should all agree on moral principles. No one should be obliged to give up or even water down their religion-based morality, in order to fit in with the views of others. Nor should we assume that there is just one set of correct moral principles, internally consistent and capable of being proved to be the one and only set that ought to be adopted.

There is force in such objections. The belief that there is one and only one proper religious creed, one and only one set of moral principles by which everyone ought to be bound, one and only one moral ideal, all others being abhorrent, has certainly cost untold lives and caused enormous suffering, ever since the beginning of history. Moreover to speak of a consensus morality strongly suggests that this will be the morality of the majority, who will then be empowered to subject the minority to the kind of tyranny against which John Stuart Mill wrote with such passion in *On Liberty*. He there enunciated what he called a 'simple principle' that the only valid reason for not tolerating a kind of behaviour is that this causes harm to people other than the people who practise it (Mill, *On Liberty*, ed. G. Himmelfarb, Penguin Books, 1974, p. 68). According to this principle, there should be room within society for individuals or groups living in ways that other people might find distasteful, even grossly immoral, provided that these eccentrics stick to their own places, and do not attempt to make converts. No one should be told what he ought to think, or how he ought to live, even if his preferred way of life is the cause of his own destruction. It is easy to be enthusiastic about this ideal. If, as seems probable, Mill was primarily thinking of women when he wrote *On Liberty*, he certainly had good cause for his passion in 1859, when the tyranny of the majority, or consensus morality, enjoined that women must not be educated, or do any but the most trivial domestic tasks, and that if they did they would ruin their health and beauty.

When H. L. A. Hart and Lord Justice Devlin joined battle over the Wolfenden Report on sexual morality, and in particular over the decriminalization of homosexual practices between consenting adult males (H. L. A. Hart, *Law, Liberty and Morality*, OUP, 1963; P. Devlin, *The Enforcement of Morals*, OUP, 1959), it was understandable that Hart should invoke *On Liberty* in defence of freedom for the individual, against Devlin's apparent reliance on the prejudices of the Man on the Clapham Omnibus. Hart argued that society must decide, on broadly utilitarian lines, whether legislating against a practice, even if fairly widely thought wrong, would do more harm than good. And 'harm' in this context would include the restriction of individual freedom, and the possible unenforceability of the law, if it were enacted. However, a different objection commonly brought against Devlin's argument that the law must enforce the common shared morality was that there was no longer any such thing. Devlin may well have been wrong in thinking there was a consensus of horror, outrage and disgust at the thought of homosexual practices at the time that he wrote;

nevertheless, in arguing that the law must be based on an accepted morality, and must in some cases criminalize that which is generally held to be wrong (and certainly must not criminalize things that are not generally thought wrong), I believe that Devlin was fundamentally right. After all, though we live in a plural society, and we are told that different people have fundamentally different views of what is right and wrong, yet all of these different people have to live subject to one system of law. If the law strays too far from what is widely thought to be right, whether in the matter of what is to be a criminal offence, or what sorts of civil cases may be brought, or, especially, what are appropriate sentences for convicted criminals, then the law will cease to be regarded. That something is illegal will become a weaker and weaker consideration in the decision whether or not to do it. Juries will not convict, in cases where they think the law is genuinely unjust, or a mandatory penalty too high. No one ought to be fined £1,000 for dropping a crisp packet in the road, any more than he should be hanged for stealing a sheep. If so-called mercy-killings, conscientiously carried out at the wish of the patient are to be penalized by the mandatory life-sentence attached to the crime of murder, then the killings may become routine. No one will ever be found guilty. There exists a general moral sense of what is morally wrong about such harsh sentences, and where, more or less, the line should be drawn in such cases. If the law diverges too far from this common moral sense, so much the worse for the law. We cannot totally separate the criminal law, at least in its broad outlines, from morality; and this means a generally accepted morality.

Such considerations may suggest that the plurality of moralities within our society has been exaggerated. In so far as the legal system on the whole works; in so far as it is a unified system; and in so far as most people are law-abiding, because they would in any case regard it as morally wrong to do the kinds of things which the criminal law prohibits, we seem, after all, to possess a considerable number of shared moral values.

However, we should take note of certain distinctions. There are several different kinds of problems sometimes explained by the fact that society is 'plural' with regard to moral values. First, there is an increasing problem of policing, of actually controlling behaviour such as mugging, rape, theft and fraud. There is, among considerable groups of society, no general feeling against this kind of behaviour, and the police, trying to control it, are widely regarded as the enemy, as are judges who utter sentences in court. What is at issue here is not strictly a plurality of different views of what is right. It is not an outcome of a diverse society, within which there are conflicting concepts of morality. It is rather that there is, on the one hand, a concept of morality, roughly in line with the criminal law, and upon which the law is based, and on the other hand, no concept of morality at all. There are, on this side, many different passions, such as greed, racial and sectarian hatred, or lust. Such passions have always existed in human nature. Morality, where it exists, exists to combat and control them. But not all individuals have any wish to control them in themselves. Such individuals have always had to be controlled by external means, that is by the law. If such passions were not subject to control, internally by a moral sense, or externally by the forces of the law, there would be no such thing as a civilized society. Given that there is no reason to suppose that such passions will ever entirely disappear from human nature, most people are grateful to the law, in so far as they are protected by it, as potential victims. They regard the law as institutionalized morality, with sanctions which do not exist in the case of informal moral prohibitions. Offenders against the criminal law do not typically think that what they did was right (the case of mercy-killing is, of course, an exception, and there are doubtless others). At most they think it is 'all right' because they wanted to do what they did, and they have no serious idea of not doing what they want, provided the risks are not too great. If we adopt this somewhat simplistic view, according to which those who are committed to moral standards are in conflict with those who are not, I believe we can speak of a consensus morality, within the framework of which people generally trust the law, and the police, to protect and keep in place the values of society.

There is, secondly, a species of political theory that holds such institutions as courts of justice and police forces to be instruments of power (class power, as it might be, or racial, economic or male power) designed to defend the status quo

against morally legitimate rebels. Such political views may sometimes be used in defence of criminals who have never heard of
such ideas themselves. This does not in itself prove the views to
be mistaken; but there is no doubt that at present they are held
by a minority, and the simple view prevails. However, if this
kind of attitude towards the administration of justice and the
moral legitimacy of the police became more widespread, there
would be a genuine threat of anarchy. For the authority of the
courts and the processes of the law in general would be put in
question. Even if the consensus morality implicit in what I
have called the simple view were still to exist among a majority,
this majority might begin to fear that they had no powers and
no authority to keep the institutions which, on the whole, they
trust in place. (This is why miscarriages of justice, or bad
behaviour and corruption among the police, constitute so powerful a threat: they undermine that trust which is essential to the
simple view.)

Thirdly, there is a different category of problems that may
arise in the relation between the law and morality which reflect
a genuine clash of moral principles. Such cases are comparatively rare. The issue of abortion is one of the most obvious of
such cases. (Another instance is that of the use of animals for
research.) Here there is apparently no hope of moral agreement,
one set of people holding that abortion is always (or almost
always) absolutely wrong, and that any law that is not totally
prohibitive is not just inadequate, but itself a moral evil. Extreme anti-abortionists hold that abortion is murder, in that it
is the deliberate destruction of human life; and whether they
defend this view on the grounds that the fetus has a right to
life (which is probably the most generally adduced ground, in
any country which has a Bill of Rights) or whether on the
ground that murder is intuitively abhorrent, they can argue that
no legal system which condemns murder can properly condone
abortion. These extremists are doubtless a minority; but while
they hold their opinions with such passion, it would be misleading to speak of moral consensus in this context.

To continue with the instance of abortion, the arguments
of those who have been responsible for the present relatively
permissive law in this country have been on the whole utilitarian, as are the arguments of those who live happily under

the laws. It has been argued, for example, that prohibitive laws do not prevent the occurrence of abortions; and that under them, 'back-street' abortions led to frequent deaths which no longer occur. It is further argued that, weighing up the wishes of the mother against the putative wishes of the fetus, the mother's wishes must have priority, since she is a person who has been born, with a life in which she is fully engaged, while the fetus is not. Such arguments, while leaving it for individuals to follow their own conscience about whether they personally will seek an abortion or carry one out, nevertheless strive to defend a notion of what will be best overall. It is indeed such an attempt to gauge what is a common good that must lie at the foundation of all legislation. In such issues as abortion the law does not so much reflect an already existing consensus morality, for such a consensus does not exist. It rather seeks to impose one. Legislators in such cases must ask not 'what is absolutely right?' but 'what is for the best?' or 'what will work?'

There is an important respect in which such legislation still rests on consensus morality. Given that it is impossible to legislate on such an issue as abortion in a way that will satisfy everyone (it is an issue on which compromise is hardly possible) there must nevertheless be a presumption that even those most dissatisfied will so far respect the law that they will use only legitimate ways to try to change it. Since no one is compelled to have an abortion or to carry one out on someone else, no one is being required to do something, as an individual, which would go against a strongly held moral principle. But the law still applies to those individuals; and the only weapons to use against an existing law are the weapons of persuasion. There is, then, in the abortion issue, and other relatively few genuine conscience issues, at one level no consensus and not much hope of achieving one in the foreseeable future, though dialogue will continue. At another level there is a general consensus that the law is to be upheld, and that no one should be prevented by violence from benefiting from its provisions. It would be absence of consensus at this level, with the consequent recourse to violence, that would put civilized society in jeopardy and render government impossible.

Moral values may thus influence our lives at various levels, both publicly and privately. If the rule of law is to be upheld, and society therefore to be tolerable, then there must be a shared determination that this shall be so; and this strong wish or determination is something that we must be prepared to pass on to children, so that they can absorb and understand it. As I have said, values are not simply accepted automatically. They have to be taught. But a belief that the law should be upheld is not enough. What the law enjoins or prohibits as a whole must be felt to reflect a system of moral values broadly accepted by those who are subject to it. This cannot be understood by children unless they are taught that there are such things as moral values that apply to themselves individually, and that the world can be properly understood and given significance only in the light of them.

It is becoming increasingly difficult to engage the imagination of children in moral, as opposed to other values, such as those of various kinds of pleasure or satisfaction. This is partly a matter of the particular vocabulary of morality that we have at our disposal. Words such as 'conscience', 'duty' or 'virtue', even the names for particular virtues such as honesty, truthfulness or loyalty, have all become suspect and embarrassing. A century ago, even if people were not noticeably religious, they were most of them familiar with some form of liturgy within which such concepts as 'sin' and 'temptation' had meaning. Today this is not so. But the absence of religion is by no means the whole explanation of our uneasiness with the language of morals. We have lost our readiness to ascribe responsibility to people for their own behaviour; we are more thoroughly prepared to think of their behaviour as conditioned by their environment, or as the inevitable expression of their DNA. We are also far more nervously egalitarian, afraid of setting ourselves up on the high moral ground, to be what is said to be 'judgemental'. To make moral judgements, in fact, is thought to be something we none of us have any right or any authority to do. For these and other reasons the task of introducing children to the idea of morality is extraordinarily complex.

Yet morality must come through education; and this entails a responsibility for teachers. Indeed, as we are now increasingly told, there is no part of a teacher's duty that is more important than the teaching of morals. It seems to me that there are two ways that teachers may go about this part of their task. First, they should be bold in their use of moral language when faced immediately with instances of what they know to be morally bad behaviour. They must pluck up their courage, when intervening in cases of bullying, cheating, theft or violence, to use the word 'wrong' (or perhaps 'cruel' or 'dishonest'). The teacher must not be afraid to show himself morally outraged by such behaviour. School is an arena for moral transactions, and often nursery school is the place where a child first learns both that there are others in the world besides himself who must be taken into account, and that there is such a thing as authority, commands that must be obeyed, kinds of behaviour that are absolutely ruled out, for ever. In the classroom, the teacher must be a moral absolutist, a 'cognitivist' who knows what is right, and is determined to see right done. The values this teacher is upholding are those about which, as I have argued, there is consensus within society. It makes no difference whether half the pupils in the class are Muslim, half Christian; it makes no difference what the cultural background of the pupils may be. There are moral values that can be taught here which are cross-cultural, and which have existed to be upheld as long as humans have lived in society at all.

The second method available to teachers arises more directly out of the argument of the foregoing chapters. Morality is not the only set of values that exists. There are many other aspects of life that can be discovered by the imagination which are intrinsically valuable to humans, and which give meaning to human life. Any one concerned with educating children, whether at home or at school, must attempt to get them to recognize and begin to understand things wider and still more fundamental than moral values, those more general values such as love and hatred, fear and confidence, creativity and intellectual excitement, curiosity and the wish for truth. These are values which we share with other humans, which give point to our lives, and which can be introduced to children by people who themselves manifestly regard them as worth pursuing. We can embrace such values only by the exercise of imagination, that faculty by which we see beyond the immediate object of our senses into what lies behind the immediate. It may be for the teacher to introduce a child for the first time to the idea of doing something well, getting something right, and the great satisfaction that this brings. Equally it may be a teacher who first makes a child think of some subject, or aspect of a subject, as complex and exciting and worth pursuing for its own sake. Such revelations of the imagination are of infinite importance, for they make work worth doing, indeed they make life worth living. But they cannot come without effort; and large numbers of children have nowhere but school where such imaginative effort and intellectual concentration are encouraged. A teacher of such children has a heavy responsibility. If their imagination is not engaged, they will never see any point to what it is that they are required to do. They will remain outside the system of shared values which hold together the other passengers in the human boat. They will in fact be in that boat with the rest, but will be unable to understand what it is that binds the rest together, and makes the voyage worthwhile.

I have suggested that one of the ways in which the imagination is engaged and values are uncovered is through the telling of stories, of all degrees of sophistication. The importance of this story-telling cannot be exaggerated as part of education. I believe, for example, that it is central to a child's education that he should learn the stories of religion (and especially in this country of the Christian religion), not just because they form part of that historical culture of which I have already spoken, but because they stand as metaphors of values that the child may thereby come to understand and share. Indeed, he may come to see these stories as the only vehicle in which such values can be expressed (or may understand how other people have come to feel this to be so). Equally, the child must learn to tell himself the story of his own life; to understand the significance of what he remembers, and to articulate it, as part not only of his self-knowledge, but his sympathetic knowledge of other people, the people he has known all his life. He must learn to give his life a shape, as all story-tellers do, not live it unreflectingly, like other animals.

If we can educate a child's imagination, we will give him a place in time. We will allow him to stretch his sense of the present back into the past, both his own individual past, and the past of the world as a whole. But we shall also free him to contemplate the future, his own, and that of the world. It has been my contention that, through this sense of continuity which we can achieve by imagination, we may find that there are values that endure, if not unchanged forever, yet recognizably persisting into the present and the future. It is fashionable these days to insist that children at school be taught, as they say, 'the difference between right and wrong'. It is sometimes implied that this is a lesson that can somehow be added to the rest of the curriculum, and that there will come a time when the teaching can stop, because the child will have learned the lesson. Nothing could be further from the truth. The internalizing of this, or any other value, the adopting it as something to aspire to and live by, can be the outcome only of a long, and indeed unending, imaginative exploration of how things are. How things are, as I have said, involves, as well, both how they were, and how they will be. We shall not get, or even approach towards, the society we want unless we take seriously this aspect of education, and make it central.

Index